Further Praise for

My Mother's Autobiography

"Payne, whose 2013 memoir *Speaking to My Madness* described her path through schizophrenia with stunning elegance and lucidity, now tells the same story (fictionalized) through the eyes, sensibility, and voice of her mother.... I have seldom found a character simultaneously so exasperating and deserving of good fate."
—David Dobbs, *New York Times* contributor and author of *My Mother's Lover*

"Dr. Payne writes with an honesty and openness that allows the reader to feel what she is feeling and experiencing, as her mother struggles to become the person she wants to be."
—Nancy Gary, PsyD, Family Therapist and Founding Director of the Piton Foundation

"*My Mother's Autobiography* deftly explores the social norms of our mothers and grandmothers in a way that is entirely relevant to our modern times. Payne's novel shimmers with introspection. I'll read this book again and again."
—Windy Lynn Harris, author of *Writing & Selling Short Stories & Personal Essays*

"*My Mother's Autobiography* delivers the searing story of a family caught at the crossroads of mental illness, social climbing, and family hurt. With raw and moving language, Payne explores the wounds we inflict on ourselves and our loved ones, and she navigates these truths with vigorous sincerity. Payne confronts the prejudices of early classifications of mental disorders, while pushing the boundaries of autofiction into new and exciting territory. *My Mother's Autobiography* is an absolute triumph of storytelling."

—Andrea Bobotis, author of *The Last List of Miss Judith Kratt*

My Mother's Autobiography

A NOVEL

By
Roberta Payne

© 2024 copyright Jaded Ibis Press

First Edition. All rights reserved.

Printed in the USA. No part of this book may be used or reproduced in any manner without written permission from the publisher, except in the case of brief quotations embodied in critical articles or reviews. For information, please email: info@jadedibispress.com.

ISBN: 978-1-938841-31-6

Cover and interior book design: Nicole Roberts
Cover art illustration: Nicole Roberts

This book is available in paperback and electronic book format.
Payne, Roberta

My Mother's Autobiography / Payne

In memory of my beloved friend and mentor
Deborah Levy, PhD
The School of Medicine, Harvard University

May her memory be for a blessing.

1

One afternoon in June of 1952, Len arrived home in a brand-new, white Lincoln Continental sedan. It was huge, with sleek curves that breathed: "Money, lots of money."

I walked to the driveway, confused. What was this doing here, all of a sudden? Whose was it, and why was Len driving it?

"I bought a *real* car. This is the finest machine ever built by Henry Ford," Len said.

He grinned, leaning against it in his blue-striped overalls, his hand on its shiny roof.

Two years before, Len had begun talking again about becoming a millionaire, just like he had back at the BF Goodrich factory in Akron. Now, here in Denver, Len was sure he had found a guaranteed way to become rich. He'd bought five pairs of brand-new Speed Queen washers and those wonderful new machines—dryers—and installed them in the basements of five apartment buildings. Shiny and white, a pair of Len's appliances would cost the housewives who lived in those apartments a dime to wash and a nickel to dry per load. Twenty percent of the money would go to the owner of the building, and the rest to Len.

It was pretty easy money and the washers and dryers multiplied, as did the money he was taking in. Success went straight to his head. He took up smoking Cuban cigars that came in glass tubes, and he bought the first television set on our block. Now this.

"You WHAT?" I asked. "You didn't ask me? Are you telling me that?"

"It's my money."

Chin up, head back, I hissed, "Get indoors. I don't want the neighbors to hear what I'm going to say."

Just inside our bungalow's little living room with its make-do furniture, I slammed the door and whirled around on him. "You didn't take me with you?"

"This is the one I wanted."

I stepped right up to his face. "Len, Len!"

Mouth open, he looked—of all things—surprised that I was upset.

The girls appeared. Leah stared wide-eyed at me and then at her father and burst into tears and started screaming. Her bushy, black hair stuck to her face, wet with tears. Then Jane, who looked like a child movie star with long dark-brown hair and natural poise, ran up and hugged Len's waist like she was saving him from me.

"You'd just go and ruin this for me, wouldn't you?" he shouted above their noise.

"Len, you have a family, you have a house."

"I can pay for the goddamn car."

"That's not the point. You don't understand. We come *first*. A man's finest asset is his wife and children. We depend entirely on you as a man."

"YOU don't understand. You sound just like your screaming girls."

"Don't talk to me like that. I'm your wife."

He laughed and pulled out the stub of the cigar he had in his back pocket. I didn't know what he meant with that.

"Daddy, Mommy says you can't smoke in the house," Leah shouted, fear of both of us in her high, shrill voice.

"You girls go to your room." Len always said that when he could barely stand them.

I whispered, "It's all right, Jane, it's all right, Leah," just so I could have the last word.

I could see he was getting ready to walk back out the front door, all dramatic, so I beat him to the end of the argument. "Okay—I'm going to our room. When I come back out, I want that car *gone*."

Lying alone on my bed, I asked myself, *What kind of woman would want her husband dead?*

Just then, I didn't care, and I didn't care how it happened.

Dead.

But what would I do if something really did happen to Len?

Out here in Denver, no one would help, except neighbor ladies bringing me casseroles. Len's brothers and my brother would help, but they were in faraway Ohio. That meant I'd have to move back there. Perhaps because it was summer, I found myself remembering thick green Midwestern grass, lush trees, and summertime fireflies the girls could play with, catch in jars. Jane and Leah could run in little herds, in all the greenness, with the cousins they'd never met.

I paused at that cozy thought because, quarreling loudly at each other, two brown squirrels raced across my backyard right up to my open bedroom window. Then they turned and disappeared.

I went back to my reverie, suddenly aware of the consequences of Len's hypothetical death.

How does a woman sell a house and move across the country? Slick real estate agents, men with big smiles—they'd try to take advantage of me. I imagined myself pushed to make decisions I couldn't understand. To pack up my dishes, with two daughters underfoot. And just leave objects behind.

But I couldn't live with my parents; my mother's heart had become bad. She rested all day, walking slowly through the old house in Germantown. Small children with all their energy could cause her to have a heart attack, maybe die. Even well-mannered children like mine.

I couldn't move in with Len's parents on the other side of Akron. They were too poor. The homestead house, standing on piles in the dirt and mud, was so old it sagged under the living room. And anyway, Len's mother had cancer in her breast, so for her it was really only a matter of time.

It all boiled down to this: I would need a man here, in Denver, who would take care of a plain woman with two small girls. How unlikely. I was searching around in my mind when I suddenly realized who could: Dr. Osborne. Of course! He had been my doctor ever since we'd moved here. He had stature, solemnity. Yet he smiled. He had a slightly gray, clipped mustache, and hands that moved toward me, around me as he spoke. He listened, and cared. These days he was watching me in case I developed a heart condition, like my mother. He said they run in families. Dr. Osborne would be there for me.

It was a deeply satisfying daydream. As I lingered over it, Len made the next move. He came in our room without knocking. I didn't know what was coming. I was lying flat on my bed, staring out the window at the great big cottonwood trunks in the backyard. I didn't turn my head to him, but in my mind's eye, I could see his ruddy face, now probably really red.

I muttered in a tired voice, like I'd been suffering deeply, "Did you take it back?"

"No, I did not take it back, and I'm not going to take it back. And that's the end of the conversation."

"You're going to make me have a heart attack," I said, eyes closed. I turned my head to the wall.

"Good, go ahead and have one."

He'd never said that before. Perhaps he wanted me as dead as I wanted him.

"Shut your trap—now," he demanded. "Get up and go feed those girls, *stup*."

Stup, he'd said. *Stupid*. What I was poured over me—an ugly, immigrant, female who only had girls.

I got up off my bed, straightened my apron, and jerked the bedroom door shut behind me. It came close to hitting his thigh. Or his front, if he'd turned around to follow me, which would have served him right.

He didn't come out for supper.

I went to the girls' room. Wild Leah and ladylike Jane, both were lying on their beds, knees drawn up like they were embryos.

5

The three of us had grilled-cheese sandwiches, which Len loved. I could imagine him lying there on his bed, smelling them. That served him right, too.

Then Jane, Leah, and I went out to the sofa and read about stupid wild animals in *The Jungle Book* and watched George Burns on the television set. Jane and Leah, on either side of me, mewed all evening. Leah rubbed her face until the allergy sores on her mouth were bleeding. Jane pulled out eyelashes and picked at her trembling lips. When they got so worn out that their hands lay still at their sides, Leah's head in my lap and Jane's against the corner of the sofa, I put them to bed, wiped secret tears, and told them I loved them.

Jane said, "I want my daddy."

I went into our bedroom and told Len I would not tolerate his spending the night there.

Without a word he left.

The room smelled like cigars, not that he'd been smoking in there, but because *he* smelled all over like cigars.

I guessed he'd spend the night sleeping in his brand-new, white Lincoln Continental sedan. All that white metal reminded me weirdly of a washing machine. But Len, he was Mr. Big Shot.

2

I dressed the girls and myself up, and we took the trolley to the Denver Dry Goods Company, downtown. It was a big, white, five-story building on Sixteenth Street. When we got there, I let Jane say, "Cosmetics, please," to the elevator lady, who wore a black uniform, a black hat with a tiny veil, white gloves, and red lipstick. She sat on a little seat inside the elevator.

I was angry. Angry that I had to try again to be attractive, after all these years. Wearing cosmetics was like begging. Begging my big shot husband to see me as a woman instead of just a wife who made the meals and did the laundry in his shiny, white Speed Queen washer. Who patted me on the head when I tried to hold hands or slip my arm under his. He had never once, in all these years, gotten me flowers or brought me a cup of tea while I was in bed.

"Cosmetics" was a whole section of the second floor. Rows of glass cases showed off little boxes and tubes of creams and lotions, and intimidating bottles of amber-colored perfume. Smartly dressed, authoritative women stood behind the counters.

I should have been the authoritative one, now that my husband was a white-collar worker. He wasn't just making money with his Mile-High Washing Machine Rental, no, now he was also a flight dispatcher for United Airlines. He wore a tie and suit to work, the only man on our block to do so. Classy—that was the word I'd use.

It had been so long since I'd bought makeup that all the brand names, except Maybelline, were new to me. I told the cosmetics lady that I wished to purchase the basics: rouge, powder, eyebrow pencil, and lipstick. I didn't get perfume because that smell was just cheap advertising. Anyway, I was allergic to it.

"I want to be a lady and wear perfume someday," Jane said, her eyes full of dreams. She was eight years old now, and so dainty she would smooth down the tiny wrinkles in her skirt every time she stood up.

"Well, I'm a lady, and I don't wear perfume," I said.

"I mean a real lady. With long golden hair."

I wondered if airline stewardesses had long golden hair. I tried to imagine the whole glamorous world of air travel in 1957. Charles Lindberg and Amelia Earhart were still national heroes, but now flying was for everyone. When Len had applied for a job at United Airlines, their Denver office had given him an aptitude test, and found him mentally quick. So, important men in suits and ties had trained him over several months to be a flight dispatcher who, wearing his own suit and tie, would analyze weather for the pilots. Now he was working with cloud systems thousands of feet above him, temperature extremes, unheard-of speeds and distances. He actually talked over a telephone several times a day with dispatchers as far away as Chicago.

The woman behind the glass counter had a power to her that reminded me of female doctors— like the girls' Dr. Gardner—who would finger point against authoritarian mothers. Meaning me, I was sure.

This attendant picked out a shade of rouge and rubbed it into my cheeks with her index finger, penciled my eyebrows, and dabbed pale powder on my big nose with a white puff. I cringed while she peered at my nose as she worked. She held her hand-mirror up so I could try the red lipstick. My lips had always been too thin, and now they became *two* thin bright lines, like those on a Japanese doll. The woman gave me instructions on how to paint "curved, sensuous lips," the kind my husband would admire. How condescending. Well, since she worked, she probably didn't have a husband.

But I did. And he'd been found worthy of enormous responsibility, and it was heady. His eyes twinkled and his lips crinkled in a smile whenever he talked about his place in the company, his place as a professional. Surely he thought back to the boys still in the rubber pits of Akron.

Maybe Len actually loved United Airlines. Len in love.

But he didn't love me.

Painted, I stood back and looked around at the scores of elegant ladies enjoying their shopping, talking among themselves, pointing at this and that, carrying bags with new purchases. My anger faded to bewilderment, and I hoped someone would somehow notice me among all the happy wives.

On the trolley ride home, I felt my cosmetics hang loosely on my face, like frosting on the side of a cake. Jane and

Leah kept smiling at each other like they had a mutual, secret joke about me.

Just before we all sat down for dinner, I took the ham slices out of the oven and then went to the bathroom to apply some fresh rouge and powder, and of course, the lipstick. Len could hardly wait, because he loved ham with yams and a sweet sauce with chunks of pineapple and bell pepper. He may have glanced up at the big, white casserole while I was serving, but he didn't notice me. He did not notice me. He did not notice the rouge, powder, penciled eyebrows, bright lipstick. Not while we ate, not while I cleared the table. He went out to the front porch to smoke his cigar. I imagined circles forming tight chains around my feet, my neck—even making handcuffs—and never figuring out what any of them meant.

Monday was my laundry day, Tuesday my shopping day. One Wednesday, while the girls were at school, I took off my apron, combed my hair, and walked around the corner of the block to knock on the door of Mrs. Creighton's bungalow.

I was thirty-nine years old, and I wanted to see if the life of a divorcee was better than mine.

I didn't know what I'd see. I'd never been in the house of a woman like that before. Would she be wearing black high heels and a long silk scarf, even though it was the middle of the morning? Then what would I say?

I hadn't invited her over for coffee cake when she'd moved in a year or so before. I'd waved at her over the chain-link fence dividing our backyards, but it hadn't seemed right to do more. Patty and Sandy, her little blonde daughters, were about the same age as Jane and Leah. The four girls played together often, but—I realized now—only in Mrs. Creighton's backyard and home. Her girls didn't come in our house.

Anyway, Mrs. Creighton came to the front door. It was open, no doubt to let fresh air in through the screen. Just like mine. She had on periwinkle pedal-pushers, penny loafers, a white cotton blouse with a little rounded collar, and a checkered apron. Her brown hair was short and tousled, like mine. She wasn't even wearing lipstick. We stared at each other. I was struck by how small she was. And to think I'd been afraid of her, like the "stews" at United Airlines: all dressed up and statuesque.

She opened the screen door.

"Mrs. Hope. It's so good to meet you. Can you come in?"

Inside, I glanced around. No brand-new furniture, no antiques either—just everyday things, a plain wooden rocker, a cloth-covered sofa. And she was tidy—no toys or games out, no books strewn on the floor.

Mrs. Creighton invited me into her kitchen: small, with a little kitchenette. Like mine. She pulled out a chair for me at the metal table, which had a pretty green tablecloth, and she poured me a cup of coffee. She brought a Danish from her breadbox and cut it in two for us.

Today was her laundry day. A divorcee doing laundry, just like a wife would—imagine that. We fell to talking about starching little girls' crinolines, and then about Sandy, Patty, Jane, and Leah themselves, because those were, really, the only subjects that were comfortable.

I looked at her ironing piled on the kitchen counters, the ironing board in front of the sink. Dresses, hers and the girls'. There were no white office shirts to iron, no man's socks to pair. No man's handkerchiefs to iron and fold and iron again until they were little flat squares. No ties to check for spots. No trunks to fold and stack.

A fresh breeze bounced through the open back door and in from the open kitchen window. There was freedom in this little kitchen.

Envy shot through me. I could be like her. I really could.

Then Mrs. Creighton's phone rang.

She listened, frowned, and turned away so I couldn't see her face. "Yes, the alimony check finally arrived. It did, yesterday. Yes. I can pay you the rent now."

So I went back home, to all its implications. But I would throw the cosmetics away.

3

We bought the ranch in 1953. Eisenhower had become president, and the country was booming. It was the right time to make a major investment. Len could see that part of it. The ranch was hidden away in the Rocky Mountains of Colorado. We got to it by three dirt side roads off the highway, two with wooden cattle guards and the last one with a metal gate.

It was summer, but the colors all around were nonetheless pale. The sparse grass in the meadows was light green, as were the pastel aspens with their white bark. Even normally red fairy trumpets were light pink here, perhaps because of some deficiency in the soil. Pastel-blue petals of the columbines matched the earliest morning sky. Butterflies were small and white. At nine-thousand feet, even air seemed pale.

I used to think of springtime as the season of the soft colors. But here spring was the time of the big snowstorms. Eight or so months of snow were followed by a short, warm, pale summer. After summer, meadow grass became dry tan stalks. Aspen leaves turned yellow, and the snow returned.

In the wilderness, winter decided everything, because there was little time for recuperation from one to the next. Animals' lives were hard.

I watched all this.

At the beginning of June, Len signed the papers to buy the ranch. Then he signed the deed legally over to me. Yes, to *my* name. This had been my idea all along, and fortunately it made sense to Len; if something should happen to him, at least the girls and I would have a place to go to immediately. With the ranch, I wouldn't have to move back to Akron and start typing again at BF Goodrich, while the girls whispered around my frail mother.

Imagine that; I was the owner of a one hundred acre *ranch*. I didn't know any other woman like me.

But Len didn't seem to care much about any of that. At the age of thirty-nine, he was still strong, probably because of the hard physical work of moving washing machines and dryers around onto his truck and into basements. So almost immediately after the signing, he got a saw with a six-foot handle. He sawed off all the dead branches on the ponderosa pines around the ranch's cabin, maybe a hundred trees, and hauled those branches off to the dump at the edge of the meadow, in his baby-blue Ford pickup. Then he raked the brown needles under the trees into big piles and hauled them away, too. I remember the sweat against his reddish complexion. It was speckled with dust from the dead needles. The top of his head sweated too, making his curly black hair glisten and curl even tighter. He spat and spat.

The next weekend, Len piled pink quartz rocks in the back of his truck, with which the previous owner had lined the driveway and the little dirt walkway up to the front door of our new cabin. We'd all laughed at them, because they looked cheap and pretentious, especially here in the middle of nowhere.

Len fenced in the immediate area—about an acre, I would guess—with metal posts and barbed wire. He built a plywood outhouse and painted it forest green to blend in with its surroundings. In July, when he took his vacation from United, he painted the trim of the cabin forest green to match the outhouse. Then he laid linoleum (white with little red splotches) on the floor of the big kitchen and the living room, which together formed a long rectangle. The sleeping porch was long too, with two big beds, complete with brass bedposts. At either end, Len added two smaller beds for the girls.

He took us all to Sears and bought every manner of wool blankets, wool jackets, and leather boots for the winter ahead. Then he returned to his job at United Airlines, and also to signing up new apartment buildings for the Mile-High Washing Machine Rental. I'm not even sure he ever stopped in his tracks to survey what he'd accomplished.

Len had to work continuously, because if he was still for a moment to look around him, the pain of being alive would have seared him and he couldn't have stood it. He had to work like that or go crazy.

I was the only person who ever understood that. Even when he was smoking his cigar late in the evening, whether on the porch in Denver while watching the sun set over the Rocky Mountains to the west, or on the patio in front of the cabin watching a log fire, he was always planning, always staring far away into his projects, oblivious of me and the girls. That's why

I had him buy the ranch. He had to be certain he'd never run out of work.

Len's father was an alcoholic, as were three of the old man's brothers, and those three brothers died of it. Len had all that desperate longing in his blood, too. But what he longed for was work.

And as for Jane, Leah, and me, every part of our lives changed too; the ranch took them over. The girls and I were soon in constant motion between Bellaire Street in Denver and Conifer Junction there in the mountains. We stayed "home" only so they could go to school and I could do shopping and laundry. Every weekend and all summer, we were at the ranch, the three of us.

Len bought me a gun. It was black and dangerous looking. I didn't want anything to do with it, because after all, you used those things to kill people. But Len said, "Look. Only one woman and two girls. You need a gun." He taught me how to load it with bullets and how to aim it with both hands. I wondered how he knew about things like that. We put it on top of the tall cupboard in the kitchen. Everybody knew it was there, but nobody ever mentioned it.

The year after we bought the ranch, we gave the girls horses—to Jane a fancy chestnut mare, and to Leah a laid-back gray mare, because she loved to ride without a saddle, sometimes even without a bridle. A pilot friend of Len's, who knew all about horses, got the two mares for us. Jane and Leah were probably the whispered envy of the other girls back in their school, and I was amazed that I was the mother of girls who had their own horses.

Len came up whenever he had weekends off from United. I had been right; it was the exactly correct setting for his soul. He thrived there. I knew where my husband was. Not every woman could say that. But I knew mine would always be there with me. Oh— I meant with the ranch.

Didn't I?

One day, Len was outside, fixing or making something. I was in the cabin, washing and drying the dishes from our big noonday meal. I pretended Len had a thirty-foot-long stapler that he was pinning everything down with, right and left, just the way he wanted it.

I looked out over my sink and saw the backwoods. Black squirrels leapt through ponderosa pines. They were smaller than the brown ones in the cottonwood trees outside my bedroom window in Denver. But both kinds were electrical, motionless one moment, the next whipping their fat tails up and down, as though the tails were doing their thinking.

I put on my brown leather jacket—it was the end of summer, and a bit nippy—and headed outside, due north, into the woods. The woods weren't pale or delicate like the meadow and the aspen groves. Instead, they were deep browns and dull greens. Their trees had hard masculine smells, both the sap and the green needles rancid and oddly sweet at the same time. A different, more musty odor rose from under my feet—long ponderosa needles; shorter Douglas fir and blue spruce needles, all dead and brown and turning back to dirt; dark piles of wild animal dung, their stale smells on the rich, heavy air. Here and there old pine cones, some round like apples, others long cylinders like half-smoked cigars.

At first, my shoes crunching the needles was the only sound I heard. Then I stopped, becoming aware of the squirrels chuckling around me, and blue jays somewhere above. And then crackling, thick-footed plodding and branch-breaking. Jane and Leah's free-grazing mares emerged from deep in the woods. They stopped, considering me with wide eyes. I clapped and spat "Boo!" They quickly turned back and disappeared.

I kept walking, and after ten minutes it was darker—the middle of the woods. There was a different kind of air here than I was used to, somehow thicker, secretive. I felt completely out of place. If it had been nighttime, I would have been afraid. Even then, in midafternoon, I wanted to look over my shoulder.

Half an hour later, I'd walked all the way to the back of my property, where the homesteaders' fence still stood. It was three strings of rusted barbed wire tacked to sturdy trees. An ancient, red-and-white metal sign on one of them said: "NO HUNTING & NO TRESPASSING."

I decided to slip through the fence to the other side. I bent down and eased a leg and my torso between the middle and the top wire (careful not to snag my leather jacket on the top one) and then I pulled my other leg through.

I walked on, in someone else's part of the woods. Here it didn't feel like "mine" any longer, but "theirs." *What?* I'd been assuming that I actually owned my piece of land: the big owner of a little ranch. I thought of the dust rising from the dead needles as I stepped on them, the compost beneath the needles, the dirt, and the granite juts below the dirt, with their bands of pink and white quartz, their green and red dry lichen. I thought of the pioneers and the homesteaders at the turn of the century, and before them the Ute Indians, now utterly gone except for the flint and obsidian arrowheads that Jane and Leah would find and bring to me. How could I be the owner of all that?

I heard a jay. Only I heard that jay. I didn't know why, but that made me wondrously important.

Then I saw the back of a tiny log house. I walked up to it. It was made of skinned pine trunks—blond, smooth, and shiny. Through the glass window I spotted an oil lamp on a wooden table. And a cot with an Indian blanket.

Loveliness washed over me; it was like a forest cottage in a fairy tale, ventured upon by a wandering child. I walked all around it, then sat on a large rock on the edge of the little clearing. Pleasure filled me, a secret, hidden gift to me alone.

I could have stayed there all by myself, with books and an orange to eat. I could have lain down on the cot, cozy. If Len had called out from our own cabin, I surely couldn't have heard him. There would have been just me, and I felt a kind of safety.

I would tell no one else. Perhaps Jane and Leah had come across it in their rides and kept it as *their* secret. I smiled at that.

As I threaded myself back through the fence wires and then headed toward the darkness of the mid-forest, I recalled, oddly, the rubber factory—back when Len and I had worked there. It was open twenty-four hours a day, six days a week, twenty-thousand workers.

Len himself had spent ten years in the rubber pits there. The best years of his body, when it would do anything he asked of it, glad to be moving, straining, pushing and pulling, just like John Henry's.

How could he have done that to himself, ten whole years of his one-and-only life?

Well, when he was working, he was a man. Not that he probably ever thought about it like that. Instead, it seemed to me, he had let Henry Ford stand for everything. American industry the greatest in the world: Ford's assembly line. And he had given his workers fair wages. So there was Len, the American worker in the BF Goodrich factory, living his hero's dream. It was an honor and a reflection of his own character. Len had explained all of this to me several times, but I thought it was kind of highfalutin thinking. I'd reply that the Depression was just outside the doors of BF Goodrich, but inside was warm in the winter, a place to be happy.

While Len built tires down below, I worked in a big windowless room upstairs, with my friend, Claire Dougherty, who was also from Germantown. Forty girls, all of us typing as fast as we could, because the slowest one was fired at the end of each month. Claire and I sat side by side at our gray metal typewriter stands and managed quick smiles to each other across the day.

We swore to each other to marry only all-American men who were going to be rich someday. Then we could be ladies in long robes, who would have leisure to read fancy magazines with colored pictures. We'd have beautiful children, who'd sit at our feet as we read to them, and husbands who'd be proud of our tastefulness.

Back in Denver, I had a photograph of Len and me standing in front of the plant headquarters, below the gigantic neon sign that said, "Everything in Rubber." Me skinny, Len tall and straight and strong. I showed the photograph to Leah and Jane when they were little. The girls were sitting on the floor, and I was leaning down at them from a chair, with the photo album open.

"That's where I was when I was young," I explained.

They both stared at it silently.

Leah burst into tears. "Is that an orphanage?"

"No, dummy," Jane said. "It's a city named BF. It's in Goodrich, where Mommy and Daddy got married."

But we left that factory behind, Len and I. To become a millionaire and a lady and mother.

I didn't know how you ended up getting to places in life. I really didn't know that. I didn't know how I got to this, to examining every bit of this forest. It had no rectangular, red brick buildings with latticed factory windows. No huge machines, shining spotless floors, time clocks, rows of smokestacks pouring out oily black. No black lunch pails and the stench of black rubber you almost couldn't get off yourself.

Almost.

4

In the summer of 1956, Len decided to replace the homestead fence surrounding the ranch with a modern one. A modern fence would have substantial posts, not just cut-off branches and the trunks of trees to tack the wire to. It would be an engineering undertaking, planned and measured, with an assembly-line crew of wife and two daughters. At times like this, he was his own Henry Ford, the man in charge of a hundred acres of open potential.

Every thirty feet, Len planted a brand-new, seven-feet-tall creosoted pole: three feet below the ground, four feet above. The creosote tar smelled worse than the tire rubber at the factory had. In the stretch between the poles, he'd drive in two metal posts. Everything measured, everything level. So many poles and so many posts before lunch. So many more in the afternoon before the girls could get off work and go to their horses.

It was all hard work, but the worst of it was the hole-digging for the creosoted poles. The digging contraption had moveable steel jaws, which bored through dirt and clanged when they hit rock. Only Len had the strength to work it. Sometimes it took an hour to dig a hole, and each time Len pulled the digger back out, one of the girls had to get down flat on the ground and put her arm in that hole to grasp and bring up dirt and pebbles and even sizeable rocks. Young girls on the ground like that, digging, their rear ends sticking up. Len probably never even noticed how angry Leah got.

The ranch had found us, lured us into buying it, and pulled us into itself. All except Leah.

I always knew Leah would leave the land, leave the hard work, the omnipresent smell of her father's sweat. For years now, he'd look at her, and then look quickly away. He didn't like her because she stalled at the hard work. When he called her a goldbricker, hurt would show all over her face, but she still avoided what work she could.

Whether he disliked her instead because she was testament to his capacity for violence was something I wondered about. An incident had happened when she was eight, in our living room in Denver. Jane must have been in her room or the basement. Leah was taunting us, yelling "I hate you!" first to me then at her father, because I wouldn't let her slide down the banister beside the stairs to the attic. Len lost control of himself and beat her up. She screamed as he threw her into the sofa, pulling her to her feet by her shoulder and hitting her across the face, stinging her again and again with his belt, all the while yelling, "Goddamn you anyway!"

It all happened so fast, so many arms and legs were flailing around, that all I could do was yell, "Len, not so hard, not so hard!" Every time I brought that up afterward, in some argument between us, he'd be quick to say, "But she was being so obstinate …" Leah told me years later that she remembered her father pulling his belt out of his trousers with a swoosh and that I was by the brown vinyl chair, but nothing about the beating itself.

Even if Leah couldn't remember, it must have been stuck somewhere in her brain, deciding her every interaction with him, even now. The summer of the creosoted fence poles, she'd be out in the barn or somewhere else far from Len while he got ready to return to Denver, his job, and the washing machine business. She stopped mentioning him when he was gone.

Then it was school time again. Physical work and riding horses in that separate world of Conifer were put aside for dresses, books, girlfriends, and evening studying. Len and I, having our own room again as we did each fall, resumed the privacy of marriage. This year in particular it did not go well, that privacy of our closeness. He and I were soon spitting the same thing at each other, over and over: *No, this is your fault. No, yours!* As the months passed, we aimed closer to the personal, vulnerable parts of each other, digging around secrets.

"I'm not here to make you happy," Len said, after one fight when the girls were away.

And he was right. He was here to support us, take care of us.

But he was wrong. There's more to marriage than that.

But he was right. He worked two jobs for us, after all. Two jobs.

Another day, Len stood back, bitter, and looked at me. "You are such a *stup*. You are as demanding as those two girls." He paused for dramatic effect, then said slowly, "If I had to do it over, I wouldn't have married."

What was I supposed to do with that?

I took my kerchief off my hair and wiped my eyes.

Those things took a toll. When school was out in June, Len and I decided he would stay away by himself for the summer. The girls and I went to the mountains as usual. I called him from the ranch perhaps once a week—stilted, fuming, short conversations, all of them. Jane would talk to her father after I did. "I miss you, Daddy. I miss you." But she didn't dare ask him to come up. Our family was a fragile egg, and it was standing on end. She knew it. All four of us knew it, one way or another.

One afternoon, when we were driving down to Field's Trading Post in the small settlement of Conifer proper, the girls and I discovered a tiny, overgrown cemetery on the dirt road just before the highway. It was so hidden that we could barely make it out from a hundred feet: mostly collapsed fence and a short row of headstones.

We stopped and walked up the little hill it was on. The wire fence drooped so low we could step over it. The thin, gnarled gray poles, really just odd pieces of pine, had rotted away at the ground, so they hung at odd angles or just lay flat. Somehow it felt wrong that a person could walk in or out wherever they pleased. A plain iron gate stood half-open, still attached to one iron pole. The crumbling gray headstones leaned toward each other in the wilderness.

Afterward, Mrs. Field down at the trading post told us it was a Mormon cemetery. So I thought, *They are far from their promised land, very far. I wonder if I am.* I'd asked for my ashes to be scattered in the aspen grove across the meadow from our cabin, among the Queen Anne's Lace. My name was Anne, after all. But whether the ranch was *my* promised land or not, I did not know.

In the middle of August, though, Len came up unannounced. The girls were gone, at the little spring down at the far end of the meadow, with their microscope.

He didn't bring me a gift. He didn't say he'd missed me.

"Is it all right if I'm here?" A whiff of snideness. He'd dared to speak, all the while looking beyond my shoulder toward the kitchen and its oak table.

"We've needed you," I said, looking at the living room floor, that white-and-red linoleum he'd put down the first summer.

Then I looked up at him, in his brown jumpsuit.

He didn't step back.

I held my hands out. "So I guess I can't live with you, and I can't live without you."

He sat down on the brown leather chair the homesteaders had left behind.

"Come here," he said.

I sat down, on his lap.

Sitting on a man's lap is uncomfortable, especially in jeans.

His hands were still at his side. I could tell he didn't know what to do next.

Leah burst in the door, smelling of horses and hay. She saw us, jerked still, and put her hand over her mouth.

"Goddamn it," Len said.

"It's all right, Len, it's all right," I said, as I had one time in Denver, years before, when she'd come in our bedroom late at night.

Len stayed.

At dinner, we had some of those little chicken pot pies from the freezer. Len ate two, he and I saying "Thank you" and "You're welcome" even for passing the salt. The girls, whose horse-smell had been disguised by the cooking, tried hard to break up the room's silence with the news in their little lives—4H, The Grange, neighbor kids who rode with them.

Then the four of us went outside to the fire pit on the patio in front of the cabin. The air was already cool. Len knelt to arrange crumbled newspaper, then twigs, aspen branches, and fir logs into a layered teepee. He reached inside it and lit the paper. The fire caught, then rose suddenly, hot and bright against our faces shining in the dark. The flames smelled of resin and wild smoke. We sat down on the sliding metal chairs, Jane between me and Len. Leah went off to sit by herself, so she could see the stars.

Neon embers popped and spit among the flaming pine logs, and a few shot upward. In the blackness above us, they floated like brilliant butterflies toward the tops of the ponderosas that surrounded the patio. Like butterflies, or lost bright souls seeking to perch on those dark silhouettes.

I looked at my hands and said to myself, *Wouldn't it be fair, really, just the two of us in all the world, just sitting here looking at each other? Wouldn't it only be fair, for him to realize that he loves me?*

To have his heart go out to me once, to know what he's missing.

I stared at the fire. An animal howled, over by the cliffs. There was no answer, but I would have if I could.

An hour of night passed while we sat in silence, our front sides warmed and toasty, our backs cold in the mountain air. I watched the flames reflect in Len's eyeglasses. He had given himself entirely over to dreams. Dreams of money, of being a big shot, of getting even for his childhood of poverty. Was there more, behind the glasses with their flames, behind the eyelashes, behind the eyelids and the hazel eyes?

There had to be more, or I would have no point beyond the girls.

As the night progressed, the burning ate at the red-hot undersides of the logs, then rose curling around them, like a mother's arms. One by one the logs collapsed, popping and spewing sparks. With his iron poker, Len broke them into crimson chunks the size of fists. Then there were only little pieces of red, like fingers, on the floor of the pit. We watched them fade.

In the black heap of ashes and burned-out splinters, a single flame quivered like a votive candle. I imagined a priest, going through his church on his last round of the night, putting out, with a quick puff, the little flames of the dead.

Len got up and pulled the big square of blackened sheet metal over the pit to suffocate what might have been left, might otherwise have somehow shot up, catch, and become a monstrous fire that would race across the tops of trees. Everyone knew stories like that.

Then the silence of four people in their separate beds, in the utter darkness of a cabin in the woods.

The next morning, I wanted him to stay. I didn't know if he wanted to or not. He split and piled up wood on the patio, enough to last the girls and me for several nights, checked the water heater and the well, and went on his way. He had two washing machines and one dryer that needed fixing, down in Denver.

He kissed me by brushing my cheek with his chin.

I stood on the patio and watched his car pull away. Then I sat down on one of the chairs in front of the covered pit and looked across the meadow, where the girls' horses were grazing, and then at the aspen and the bed of Queen Anne's Lace. I thought of my ashes, and I was bitter.

5

In a sense, Len and I went our separate ways then. Of course, we were still Mr. and Mrs. Hope. I wondered if he too, laughed privately at our name. But you reach a point where there just isn't any hope between yourselves, so you hope for children, the job, the business, the unquestionable monument of the ranch. Len and I became—to use a term popular in those days—a team. And we worked well on that tragic level, tragic only if I stopped to think about it. The girls' lives took over mine. The Mile-High Washing Machine Rental, getting bigger and bigger, took over Len when he wasn't at the ranch or at United. We all reported our vivid happenings to each other, like little births, hatchings, and hopes of more births. Almost an endless show-and-tell at our house and at our ranch. Hope was on every tongue. The girls were getting used to having enough money from their father and me that they needed to only wish out loud. Len was getting used to winning on a daily basis. I was getting used to some unconscious decision I had made—

When? Why? Above all, how?—to live with a husband who wanted little from me but no arguing.

    Jane and Leah were both tall and skinny and ready to take on the world. As they passed through their adolescence, they became interested in everything around them, all the way to the horizon and the heavens themselves. Then in a flash, Jane was in high school. She even mentioned college. I told her that when I was a girl, I was accepted to the University of Akron, but my parents were too poor to send me. I could have been a doctor. But Jane herself would be able to go to college anywhere she wanted and study anything she wanted, because we were becoming almost, well, almost *rich* with the Mile-High Washing Machine Rental. Yes, the girls could take money and, as they grew up, turn it into a grand classiness. Meanwhile, it was up to Jane to study and become accomplished in everything she did. And there were so many things to take on.

    First: books, of course. But books were already the center of their lives, right up there with horses. I'd raised them on books. I bet the other children in their school weren't cultured readers. As soon as they could read, Len and I bought them *Collier's Encyclopedia*. An investment, Len had said. I put the twenty volumes on the lowest shelf of the bookcase, so the girls could get to them first. They memorized from *The Family Book of Best-Loved Poems*. When Jane and Leah were seven and six, I sat them on either side of me on the blue sofa and read to them from the Bible—how I laughed at Eve coming from Adam's rib, and men living seven-hundred years! Perhaps I should have been reverent about all that supposed holiness, but I wasn't. When my daughters reached junior high school, when other girls were just reading *Nancy Drew* books, I joined The Book of the Month Club, and we read *Madame Curie, Jane Eyre*—both girls crying—*The Sonnets of Elizabeth Barrett Browning*, and of course, *Gone with the Wind*. Dear Claire, my friend from BF Goodrich, would have been proud. This was indeed what I was meant to do: read books with my beautiful children. However, in two or three years, the girls were beyond me. Jane read the *Iliad*, and Leah *Poems from the Greek Anthology*. I could only guess what they were about, but neither of the girls thought I would understand. Actually, I understood a lot. In fact, I discovered and understood Khalil Gibran's *The Prophet*. It was my "non-Bible," full of deep meaning, and it paid off. Although Jane made a little face at it, Leah would pick it up from time to time, because she said it made her feel dreamy.

I did so much with them, for them. The weekly round-trip to the ranch and back. To tell the truth, I was always tired, perhaps because of my heart condition. No wonder I was starting to get gray.

At the ranch, Jane and Leah had a big telescope, enameled white and about four feet long. In the summer—the nights we didn't have a fire in the patio pit—both girls liked to carry the telescope from the cabin to its black iron base down in the meadow. They'd assemble the two parts and peer at the moon and the planets through the six-inch lens. Their favorite views—other than the Moon, of course—were Mars, which really did turn out to be reddish up close, and the elegant rings of Saturn. When they had finished with the telescope, they would lie down on blankets on the meadow grass, far from manmade lights, and gaze at the Milky Way until they became cold and sleepy.

Their place among the stars.

Through the years, either at the ranch or at home, Jane and Leah had a dog, a stream of cats, mares and foals, a burro, a rooster, a lamb, rabbits, an aquarium, a duck, turtles, and canaries. Leah bragged thoughtlessly about her horse to her classmates, until one day a girl called her a snob, and Leah cried in shame.

They pressed flowers and embroidered. They painted dishes, Christmas bulbs, and life-sized murals on the walls in the basement in Denver; carved miniature dogs and ships; pasted papier-mâché piñatas and puppets; and cemented a picture-sized mosaic queen with a gold crown, and birds drinking from a bowl. They learned calligraphy and illuminating.

Jane and Leah had private chess lessons and private riding lessons. They worked clay in the gifted children's studio at the Denver Art Museum, and attended meetings of the Denver Astronomical Society. In the summer, the girls rode in gymkhanas and collected big, purple grand-champion ribbons, Leah for barrel racing and Jane for jumping. I hung the ribbons in a big picture frame in the living room at the cabin and pointed them out in pride when visitors came. My guests were awed.

Their Girl Scout leader was in Denver, their 4H leader down the road from our ranch. The two taught canoeing and lamb-raising to groups of mostly average girls, girls many of whom would likely marry just out of high school. The Girl Scout leader was the wife of a minister—so wholesome, so aware of being wholesome. Sorry for me when I said I was a nonbeliever. Both women were college graduates, but if truth be known, I expressed myself much better than they did, and on almost any subject having to do with my girls and their lives.

Why should those without gifts be the leaders? That's what's wrong with society, I thought. *That's why society plods instead of flies.*

But those two women despised the three of us. Once the minister's wife taught a whittling class in the scout troop, and Jane couldn't handle the knife properly. She said to my daughter, "Well, *someone* has to come in last." Another time, Leah won the championship trophy at a Conifer gymkhana, and the 4H leader gave it to the runner-up instead. "Leah has won enough," that woman said to my face. I turned and walked off. Well, Jane and Leah would show them all in the long run. It's the long run that counted, after all. But right now, we had more money than the other mothers and their husbands. Money and our own ranch. And my brilliant, cultured girls.

6

A year passed. It was early June at the ranch. Jane and Leah studied for the SATs, rode, and pondered endlessly where they wanted to go to college. Len came up to spend his vacation time. There was no choice in the matter, because the Rocky Mountain pine beetles were infesting our trees, had begun destroying our woods. Len undertook his hardest job ever: felling, cutting, dragging, and then burning the trees that the pine beetles had killed. There were hundreds of those trees, small and large, their bark black and their branches brittle, their once-evergreen needles now red—some in the woods behind the cabin, others in the woods across the meadow behind the Queen Anne's Lace. In the distance, on the hills and then on the mountain ranges, you could see patches of the telltale red.

Lumberjacking is sap, bark, and sawdust. And danger. Len had the spry, toothless old man from the other side of the mountain help him, because the work was too hard for our girls. The two men wore flannel shirts, overalls, thick gloves, leather boots, and caps. I just made sure they were fed and had enough water as they toiled, and I kept my mouth shut. Hard work like theirs could fly into anger, just like that.

First, Len would cut a wedge low in the tree's trunk, then he slowly drove the ripping-loud chainsaw through the wood. The old man would stand behind and over him and push the tree in a straight line away from them, so that it wouldn't twist on itself and break the chain or bend the blade or fall on them. After the tree would go down with a swoosh, cracking of branches, and a thud, Len would circle and tie it with the steel chain attached to his tractor, then pull it all the way down to the wood pile he was building in the far end of the meadow, where the ground was marshy. Then he'd drive back up to the woods and start over. The operation was as methodical and repetitive as a slaughterhouse kill line.

When the wood pile in the marsh was as tall as Len was and twenty feet in diameter, he walked around it, dousing the branches and trunks with kerosene, and then lit the bonfire. The fire's heat was frightening. As the days progressed, the faces and necks of the two men turned deep red and leathery looking. Their noses ran, and they spat right and left. The flames roared in the light summer breeze, and the air around them quivered like a mirage on a hot highway. The line of smoke could be seen down at Field's Trading Post, four miles away. The flames lasted all day and all evening. By bedtime, the bonfire was nothing but bright embers. But Len got up in the middle of each night to go check, lest the fire had secretly begun crawling across the meadow.

Each day he built the pile up and burned it down again. The Forest Service had posted flyers on the roads saying that the beetles and their eggs could be killed by fire, the infestation contained. Well, it seemed to me that some beetles would surely be knocked loose in the felling and cutting and dragging, ready and eager to infest other trees. And anyway, maybe they'd moved on from the dead trees long before, and had already bored into fresh, new victims, which at a glance still appeared healthy. But Len was usually too hot, smeared with sweaty sawdust and wood chips, and close to exhausted anger to listen to my reasoning, so I kept it to myself. Lest I be called a *stup*.

The third day in, Len made a late-morning trip to Field's. When he returned, he drove his truck up to the cabin rather than back to the barn. He got out, and I could see that his overalls and shirt were already stained, and his face red and grimy. Yet he was grinning with hospitality. He helped a middle-aged woman out of the truck's cab, explaining that she'd appeared lost, at the top of our little road. He'd stopped to help, offer her a ride.

"I'm Virginia Gunderson," the woman smiled broadly. She was quite stout, and ran out of breath walking up the short path to the cabin. I wondered where she'd come from, what with woods around us in every direction. She wore a brown straw hat, a fresh red flannel shirt, stiff new dungarees, and brown boots. With red laces! But her face was an indoors gray.

Pretending she fits in up here, I thought to myself, smiling.

"Miss Gunderson, how kind of you to come," I said, taking her hand. She had thin, sensitive hands, each with two or three rings set with several diamonds. I said, hoping to sound ladylike, "Why, Miss Gunderson, you have the hands of a surgeon."

She put her head back and guffawed. "There's nothing about me like a surgeon, except that I cost too much."

Len stood there, still grinning, with his hands in his pockets.

"Have you had breakfast?" I asked her when she sighed, her eyebrows raised, eyeing the cabin.

"Oh, I'd love something."

Indoors, she pulled out a chair at our round oak table. She didn't look around at my kitchen being readied for the day's cooking. She sat straight, waiting to be served.

Len stood back, beside the cupboard. He was smelly, and perhaps he knew it.

I fixed her coffee, toast, two eggs, and some cereal. She was hungry and ate quickly, but did not scoop or tear.

"Miss Gunderson, may I fix you anything else?"

"Oh, call me Virginia, please. All my friends call me Virginia."

"And what brings you to our neighborhood?"

"I'm renting Keuster's spare cabin for the summer. Carl Keuster keeps mentioning the Hopes, with their lovely daughters. So I was walking over to meet you."

"Well, we're very honored, Virginia."

She added quickly, "I come to Colorado every summer. I travel the rest of the year. So by June, I'm ready for quiet. How I love it here! Sometimes I rent here in Conifer, sometimes down in Evergreen, or in Aspen. Trees, trees, trees—I'll bet your husband knows about all those trees."

I glanced toward Len in his overalls, bark and sawdust clinging to them. Was she laughing at him? Did he know it? I was confused, and stepped back to my stove. I felt strangely

MY MOTHER'S AUTOBIOGRAPHY

intruded upon. I changed the subject, still smiling. "May I ask where you're from?"

"I'm from Oak Park, outside Chicago. See—another tree. It's *very* hoity-toity. It's kind of … the opposite of here. And I love both places!"

"You said you travel?"

"Oh yes, in April I went to London, Paris, and Rome. For three weeks. Well, I wasn't really *in* Rome. I stayed in a villa by the sea with some American friends of mine. That way I didn't have too much to do with the Italians. They're so noisy and rude. But I love Italy. I love the food. And I love the Americans who live there. They're always so glad to see me."

Imagine that; someone who'd been all over Europe, sitting in my kitchen.

"Well, I need to go check my fire," Len said abruptly. "It was nice meeting you."

He left. He had not sat down with us. Perhaps he was ashamed of his overalls. Perhaps he was just being rude. Or, he disliked her. But that didn't make sense.

"Len works for the airlines," I explained. "He has a very important job. He analyzes weather maps for the pilots. Most of the time he works the Denver-to-Chicago route."

"Well, I'll have to take his airplanes from now on, me and my friends." A big laugh, and a pat on my hand.

I couldn't tell if she was reaching toward me or putting me in my place. But just think—a lady, a real lady sitting in my kitchen, chatting with me.

I fed Len and the old man Eisenhower Soup at twelve noon each day. It had peas, beans, corn, little red potatoes, celery, broken-up spaghetti, and ground beef. When their meal

41

was ready, I went out on the patio and rang the black iron dinner bell, which they could hear from back in the woods, if they weren't running the chainsaw. It was a silly thing to do, a dramatic flourish, but it made me laugh because the two of them always came as fast as they could, just because of that bell. Like laboratory rats.

Every day I fed them Eisenhower Soup, I also made breakfast, bread and margarine, cookies, ice cream, and iced tea. They ate without paying me any real attention, their minds still back on their work. I stood back by the stove, looked across my kitchen now full of crusty, sticky pots and pans, and contemplated the two of them. The sun poured over them from the two windows. Len and the old man smelled like gasoline, kerosene, smoke, car oil, machinery grease, sawdust, pine resin, wood ash, male sweat, and old farts.

Surely they'd get enough of felling, dragging, and burning by lunch time, but they would never let go of it. Today, while they ate—the old man working his gums round and round—they talked about the moist black dirt, almost like a sponge, that they dragged the trees to at the far end of the meadow.

"That mud's been clogging up the tire treads all morning," Len complained.

"Makes it hard to pull a log across it," the old man said.

"After lunch, I need to go back to the barn and get some more gasoline for the saw. It needs greasing, too."

"I've got a can of grease over in my dump truck," the old man said.

While we were eating, a big, pale-blue car drove up. Len joined me at the window, looking at it. He said it was an Oldsmobile sedan, a fancy car like the white Lincoln Continental he'd brought home so many years before. Remembering the Lincoln put a big smile on his face.

Virginia Gunderson got out of the pale-blue car. I went out to the patio to greet her. Once again, she'd thought enough of us to come here. Virginia looked sporty, Pendleton shirt and a different hat now, but one of her red shoelaces had come undone and was trailing.

"Virginia, you're going to fall all over yourself and break a leg."

She bent down but couldn't reach it, because of her girth. She stood, huffing and puffing. I bent down on one knee and knotted it for her.

We went in, to the kitchen. Fortunately the men were leaving. I gathered up their dishes and wiped the table and each of the chairs.

"What in the world is Eisenhower Soup?" she asked when I offered her lunch.

"The President made it when he was trout-fishing here in Colorado. He simmers it for hours. It's a man's soup."

"Well, I liked President Eisenhower, so I'll like his soup."

She ate with the little finger of her delicate hand raised just so. "I made soup once too, in a pressure cooker," she said. "Just to see if I could do it. Well, the pressure cooker exploded or something, and there was soup all over the walls and the ceiling. The cook and his helper had to clean it all up!"

I felt for them, which didn't surprise me at all. They were likely immigrants. *I can never let Virginia know I'm the daughter of immigrants*, I thought. *Would she have made my parents clean up the soup?*

Then I was curious. "Virginia, what would you be doing right now if you were back at home?"

She looked at me and thought for a moment. "Why I might be getting my hair done. I might be getting ready to go to a ball. Just before I came here, I wore my red evening gown to my favorite ball."

I wondered about that too. Did the ladies arrive in mink coats, even though it was late May? Did they have long gloves? Did they wear tiaras? I tried to imagine the orchestra music—a gentle swing played by Negroes. Elegance.

I looked closely at her. Virginia and I had something in common; she wasn't pretty either. Her forehead was too high and her thin nose too long, and she had liver-colored lips and a receding chin. But I didn't really care, not when she threw her head back and laughed, because she didn't seem to be afraid of anyone or anything. I wished I could be gay and first class too, but who besides Virginia would ever notice?

But she'd sought me out. And she told me about her grand life. She wouldn't have told just anyone. She was enthusiastic, just like Claire Dougherty. Claire had wanted me to be part of her life, and now so did Virginia.

Len still had trees left to cut—hundreds of them—but his vacation time was over. He had no choice; he put away his tools, chainsaw, and tractor, and stomped his boots around on the ground of the last bonfire, to make sure the earth was cool, so he could go back to Denver in his baby-blue pickup truck, take a bath in a real tub and put on a suit, and then get in his car and go calculate cloud masses for the pilots flying to Chicago. Once he told us that United planes bound for San Francisco flew far above Conifer, toward the west, and that the pilots could look through their windows at the mountains below, the pale-green meadows creeping up their sides, the deep-green woods with those telltale red patches.

For the rest of the summer, down in the meadow, Jane and Leah would wave up at planes.

The day Len went back to Denver, Virginia came for lunch. She stayed the afternoon, and for dinner. She seemed so glad to be with us that I asked her to sit with me and the girls in the dark while we watched our tame little fire on the patio. I put her chair and mine closest together, and turned out the lights in the house. The single light of the fire, there in the woods, was almost holy. Anyway, that's how I felt, and I hoped Virginia would feel at home with it. But first she went to her car and came back with a sizeable, sporty canteen. She took a deep sip from the canteen and began talking. She told us about a party back home, where a maid, standing by discreetly, would drop rose petals in the toilet bowl after each guest left the bathroom. She guffawed, and I laughed too, there in the darkness. Virginia sipped; talking must have made her thirsty.

Jane and Leah, now silent, went to get ready for bed.

High silhouettes of trees around us, our eyes mesmerized by the fire, just Virginia and me.

She remarked that she felt truly happy.

"Imagine, me not rushing around."

"Why do you rush?" I asked her.

"Oh, I'm always late to one thing or another."

"You'd better watch out, or you'll end up causing an accident."

"Well, I've never done that." She sounded a little offended. "I've run over a dog or a cat occasionally, driving fast to get somewhere, but I've had to."

I shivered in the night. *Those are people's pets*, I thought.

Perhaps that is the way the rich live. Outside the realm of other living things.

Silence.

About ten o'clock, when we were cold and sleepy, I said, "Virginia, would you like to spend the night? It's too late to drive back to your cabin and go in, in the dark." She sighed, smiled gratefully, and walked over to her Oldsmobile to get a toothbrush and nightgown.

She loved us.

I thought of Jane and Leah's cat and dog, lifeless on the side of the road.

My foot was in Virginia's door, so to speak. Another world, a glittery world, one that I did and did not like.

As the summer wore on, I watched Leah's eyes light up when she heard the big car on the granite driveway. Virginia was coming! At a moment's notice, Leah would have traded her life with us—even forsaking her mare—for living out of a suitcase with Virginia.

"Have you gone to China yet, Virginia? Someday I want to see the Great Wall. I want to go all the way around the world, just like you."

Virginia laughed. "Then you'd better marry a rich husband, young lady."

Leah looked bewildered, and I didn't know whether to laugh or cry at her naïveté.

Perhaps this woman from marvelous Oak Park could—eventually—help them meet such men. After all, Virginia, had said just the other day: "Jane and Leah are like daughters to me."

Every detail was so perfect; I couldn't have made it up.

Jane was always coolly polite to her.

Sometimes Len was able to come up for a day or two now. It appeared he wrestled with his thoughts about Virginia. He got excited about money when she was here, excited about all that wealth. She made him dream his dreams bigger. Especially his dreams about the Mile-High Washing Machine Rental, someday a big company, someday a corporation. Then he'd get a big, almost angry grin on his face as her attention wandered. The anger of a working man, dismissed for his workman's overalls, dismissed by a jolly, rich woman who had never done an honest day's work. Back in Oak Park, telling servants to clean messy soup off her wall.

I bet Len imagined Virginia telling him what to do. She wouldn't have thought twice about it, and he knew it, didn't he?

When Len was back in Denver, Virginia spent nearly every day and night with us. She finally just stashed her toothbrush, nightgown, and bathrobe in the bathroom with ours. She would sip from the canteen in the afternoon and all evening. "What do you have there?" I asked her once, since the odor of whatever she was drinking was sweet and sharp at the same time.

"Oh, just a little sherry. Just a little. But I'm very fond of sherry, aren't you?"

"No, no. I'm not," I said. I'd heard of sherry but never tasted it. "But you go right ahead and enjoy it!" I smiled, bewildered but trying to sound gracious.

One afternoon, when it was just the two of us, she said suddenly, "Anne, you must come to Oak Park to visit me this fall. Let's do it next month, in September, when the weather's still good. I'll have a cocktail party just for you."

For me? That for me?

Would I have to drink sherry?

Would there be dancing? But I didn't know how! What would I say my husband did for a living? But I would smile about my girls, talk of their horses. I would say I loved to entertain Virginia on my ranch.

The cocktail party embodied my dreams, my old friend Claire's dreams, erasing completely the years in the typist pool at the factory with its sign, "Everything in Rubber."

Anne Kaiser, well, afraid—but triumphant.

I'd have to get some nice clothes. I'd go to Neusteters. The saleslady would make suggestions. I'd be grateful to her, without showing it, as though I always shopped at Neusteters. As though I always went to cocktail parties.

So I called Len in Denver. I told him about the cocktail party, and as I told him I realized Virginia hadn't invited *him*. I wondered if he'd realized that too.

"I want an engagement ring, Len."

"An *engagement* ring? You have a wedding ring."

"But rich ladies get engaged first, with a big diamond ring. Virginia's friends will want to know I'm not made of nothing." I chose my words carefully. "I want to show them that I have a wealthy husband."

Len loved that. I could tell by his silence; he savored the notion, paying his wife's luxurious way. Anne, welcomed at the open door of a mansion with white columns. "Well, yes, that would make a good investment," he concluded.

Jane, Leah, and I drove down to Denver early the next morning, and we and Len got out our best clothes. All four of us, because after all, that was the way we did everything.

Imagine us walking downtown into Bohm-Allen, the best jewelry store in Denver—all glass and mirrors, with middle-aged salesmen in suits like butlers.

The negotiation itself took place between Len and the salesman.

"We'd like to see an engagement ring for my wife."

"What do you have in mind, sir?"

Len turned to me, startled at the question directed at him.

"Something simple and elegant," I said.

"Simple and elegant. What is your price range, sir?"

"How do I know what I'm getting is real?"

"I'm afraid you'll have to rely on the reputation of Bohm-Allen." This time, he didn't say "sir."

I nudged Len with my foot.

Then I saw it, almost immediately. My diamond, there under the counter. Emerald cut, one-and-a-half carets, with an elegant gold band. It was the sort of engagement ring that people would immediately see when I walked in the door. At my cocktail party.

"Mother, get this ring instead," Leah said, pointing. "It's out of this world!" It had three diamonds in a row, surrounded in all directions by smaller diamonds. It gloated *Money, money.*

"No, Leah, no. That's not the sort of thing I would wear."

Len bought my ring. Just like that, feigning nonchalance.

"I still like the one with all the diamonds," Leah said.

"This is an investment," Len said. "The one your mother chose is the better investment."

Jane held her lips tight and walked ahead of us out of Bohm-Allen.

I did not say thank you to Len. I couldn't remember the last time I'd thanked him for anything.

My ring hand felt like a beacon. I wanted to lift it up and gesture with the diamond. I thought of Claire, how back in the factory we'd planned to marry men who'd become rich. Suddenly, I wondered if she had. Or if she'd found true love. Or both. I wondered if Len fantasized parading his wife, with her diamond ring, around the boys at BF Goodrich.

Jane and Leah and I headed back to the ranch in the early evening. I could hardly keep my eyes off the ring as I drove home with my left hand on the steering wheel. Yes, I'd wear my new diamond in front of Virginia without saying a word. I fantasized about the way she'd react.

"Oh, Anne, I never noticed your beautiful ring before," she would say. "Silly me, it's lovely.… That ring of yours is so much nicer than any ring I have.… You'll shine at my cocktail party."

Virginia came over the next day at about ten, to start the morning with some breakfast at the big oak table. She ate eagerly, but was lost in thought. I took a breath of anticipation and put my left hand on the table's edge. She looked beyond me as she said, "Oh, Anne, I'm so lonely up here. The only friend I have here is you. You don't know what it's like, over at that cabin, alone. I've made a decision, all by myself. I'm going back to Oak Park tomorrow."

"You're leaving—just like that?"

"I did most of my packing while you were gone in Denver. I'm going to finish it this afternoon, and leave early in the morning."

Trembling, I took both of her delicate hands in mine. Her rings were like the gaudy ring Leah had loved at Bohm-Allen. All I could think to stammer was, "I'll miss you so much."

"Well, I'll be back next summer. You can count on that."

Yes, that's what I could count on, for she was someone to share a dream with; I could count on that. The gall of bitterness was in my throat.

After she left, I tidied the table, automatically.

I washed down the chair she'd been sitting on.

I sat back down on mine. My face was burning with woe.

"Mother, are you all right?" Leah said, coming in the kitchen, a horse halter in her hand. "Mother? I just saw Virginia, in a hurry to get out of here. Is something wrong? Didn't she like your ring?"

"She didn't even see it."

"See! You should have gotten the big fancy one!" Leah laughed.

I could think of nothing to say.

"Are you really okay, Mother?" she asked softly.

There was Leah, caring about me. She never cared about me, about anything other than her mare, her telescope, her straight As. I wanted her to care about me because I knew she had the capacity, perhaps she alone. But today I couldn't hold out my arms in return for her caring.

I said, "There won't be any cocktail party."

Leah saw how hard that was for me. "Did you actually want to be in the same room with thirty people just like her? Come on, Mother."

"Well, you were impressed by her too."

"But Jane's right. She's not what she appears."

"What if Virginia had said to you, 'Come around the world with me?'"

"I guess I would've been totally excited. Totally."

"And if she forgot about it, then?"

Leah thought. "She'd never have the slightest idea how sad that would make me."

7

As Jane got older, I began to annoy her. She would tense and close her eyes when I blew my nose. She mocked me with a little smile when I put on my good tan dress—futile, in her eyes. But *she* was perfect. She never got a grade lower than an A, was graduating at the top of her class of seven-hundred at East High School. In the spring of 1962, Jane—our beautiful Jane with her high forehead, nose like Grace Kelly's, and thick dark-brown hair—was accepted to Stanford.

    A top university indeed. It was a gate to a shining future, and it was Jane's gate to walk through. *Imagine that*, I thought to myself. Students at Stanford were usually both rich and smart. I gleaned this from Stanford's magazine, with its pictures of chicly dressed students and notes about their summer adventures around the world. Jane knew we weren't Stanford-rich yet. But she also knew she was smart. She announced she was going to study mathematics and she might marry a lawyer, or a doctor.

Then she was boarding the plane to San Francisco—Len, Leah, and I waving goodbye. We thought we could just see her smiling face from one of those little airplane windows. Jane was the first Hope or Kaiser ever to go to college.

Len was making so much money from the Mile-High Washing Machine Rental now that he was all puffed out, able to pay his daughter's way to a rich person's school. Perhaps she would soon bring home a rich son-in-law. Len was on a different, bigger, big-shot level than he'd ever been on before, even that day when he'd bought my ring. I was amused at him, acting like a boy with a big grin. Frankly, I was kind of happy for the guy. I told him I always knew he'd end up on the top of the heap. It wouldn't really matter anymore whether Virginia Gunderson was impressed by us.

When Jane came home for Christmas, eighteen years old now and having survived her first term of college, we all went to the living room to sit and catch up. She looked tired, stooped and silent in the middle of the sofa. Len, Leah, and I stared at her.

Jane refused to show us her grades. She said she'd changed her mind, was now going to major in art history. She never called Stanford by name.

8

Nine months later, it was Leah's turn. I watched her scan the distance from under her white hat with its little starched veil. She was waiting to board the United plane which would take her to San Francisco, to Stanford, in Jane's footsteps.

Leah was tall, with curly black hair, and her dark eyes beamed with competitiveness. She'd won first place in her high school class, a National Merit Scholarship, and junior acceptance at MIT and Stanford. She chose Stanford. She was driven by hurricane energy, but she was utterly vulnerable, knocked over by the breeze of a mere comment aimed in her direction.

It wasn't that I didn't miss Jane that first year she was gone. It wasn't quite that simple, not that black and white. But with Jane gone, there in Denver it was just Leah and me, fighting and arguing. Leah had turned sullen and argumentative about the same time Jane had started being shocked by my every physical characteristic and gesture. By now, Leah sulked and then went wild, all year long. Her behavior, especially her taunts, overpowered everything else in my mind.

Soon after Jane's Christmas visit, I realized she was coming into my focus really only on Sunday evenings, when she called us collect from the public telephone at the student union. On those calls she was polite, private. I could tell she was unhappy, but I was too tired from Leah to come to her aid. For which I myself was entirely to blame, but I was too tired, really too tired.

One day, in the middle of her senior year at East High, Leah and I were arguing in her room. It was about her share of the ironing, which she'd put off and then raced through. She'd scorched two of her father's handkerchiefs.

"You don't even know how to iron, and you're going to Stanford," I said.

"That's why I'm going to Stanford," Leah laughed, her chin high.

I was embarrassed at my silly comment, but being laughed at by my own daughter was worse. "You're ungrateful and selfish, you never do your share!"

Leah made a little face. We yelled at each other.

"Your father always said you're a goldbricker, and he's right," I shouted.

"Yeah, I got into MIT and Stanford because I'm a goldbricker," she shouted back in her high, overly polished voice.

I slammed the door when I left.

After stewing about it for an hour, I was going to add the matter of her attitude at the ranch. How she'd say she had the cramps when Len asked her to help with something or other. How she'd left the lids off the grain barrels, and the mice had gotten in. I knocked on her bedroom door, but she didn't answer. So I went in. Leah was on the floor, her back scrunched into a corner, her arms around her knees, her face buried.

I went over to her and said, "Leah, Leah!" I lifted her head.

Her eyes were brilliant, staring at the wall, as though she could see past it into some distant world.

"You shouldn't do that, sit in a corner like that. Don't do it again," I said quietly, frightened by this weirdness.

Another day (I believe it was in March) I walked into her room—just because the door was open. It was a sunny day, after a spring snow. Everything was fine. But she was sitting that way again, hollow, brilliant.

I didn't tell Len. He would have just found a way to blame me.

On yet another day, Leah and I argued furiously, she baiting me as she marched up the stairs from the basement, where the washing machine was. She was carrying an empty clothes basket in front of herself. She taunted me every few steps. "We aren't like other families!"

"Other families are just like us, you better believe it," I yelled back, smacking her cheek.

She hit me back, hard across the face.

My glasses flew off.

Adrenaline rushed through me and into my heart. For a moment, I thought I would have a heart attack. Because of that vicious girl. I was stunned; I'd never heard of a daughter hitting her mother. It was as wrong as a man hitting a woman.

I slapped her face, hard.

She tripped against the basket and fell backward.

"You kicked me!" she shouted.

"I did not!"

Len had just come in from the backyard, had seen it all.

I stepped back and silently picked up the pieces of my glasses. I went to my room.

When I came out later, I poured cereal from the box for dinner.

None of us said anything.

So here she was standing on the United tarmac with her white veil. She didn't look hopeful, naïve, and moralistic like Jane had when she was boarding a year before. Leah looked like she was glad to leave us behind, even escape us—especially me. I knew that, once out of our sight, she would try to take on the world. My horrifying child, who was carrying a fancy hat box and a bright-green purse, and didn't kiss me goodbye when I leaned toward her.

When my second daughter was gone, I was —in the far-back, dark side of my brain—thrilled. I had completely unacceptable thoughts. Shocking thoughts. I pretended that I myself had actually gone to college. That I had attended the University of Akron, then gone to medical school. Anne E. Kaiser, MD. I'd never married Len, never had Jane or Leah. I'd never been a wife with the wifely duties of pleasing my husband at night and bearing offspring. I hadn't been a uterus.

I could see on my menstruation calendar, which I keep in my purse away from Len's view, the first time that I bled for ten days. When that happened again, Dr. Osborne made a tiny, sad smile. "You've begun your menopause, Anne. It may be hard, or it may not." The ordeal that women whispered about to each other, made them cling to their doctors even more fiercely—the "change of life." Would I become a different person? Be left hollow, wrinkled? But Dr. Osborne, calm at all times, was there for me.

I started bleeding in gushes. I wore two Kotexes at a time, one on top of the other. I rolled up the red pads in toilet paper to make little packages, and then burned them in the bottom of the incinerator back by the alley.

I was tired, more tired than I'd been the years I was driving those two resentful girls all over Denver and the mountains day after day, avoiding the smirks of the one and the anger of the other.

Dr. Osborne said the time would come for the hysterectomy, but later. In the meanwhile, he gave me iron shots when I saw him in the middle of each month. He would listen to my heart with his stethoscope, put his hand on my shoulder, and say, "You're handling all this well, Anne."

Len appeared to know nothing about menopause, except, I imagined, that it was sure to last for years and made women hysterical, flighty, and nasty. He must have concluded he was in for an ordeal.

One day I was in the kitchen, standing by the sink, when Len came home from United. I was bleeding hard that day. Suddenly I felt a line of blood run down the inside of my thigh, my calf. A quarter-sized circle of thick, dark-red blood appeared on the floor. I inched back and covered it with the arch of my shoe. Len saw nothing.

I was one of the fortunate women. I didn't have to wait years with a festering uterus inside me until it was bursting, until my doctor would say, "I think it's time for your hysterectomy, Anne."

I lay in bed one afternoon, too tired to get up. Dr. Osborne's gentle smile under that small, tidy moustache came to my tired mind. I recalled that I'd once said to Leah, "If anything ever happens to your father, I think I'll marry Dr. Osborne." Suddenly my hips and thighs were wet. The small of my back, too. The wetness was warm. I was bleeding to death. To death. And it would not take very long. I reached to the phone on my nightstand and called Len at the dispatchers' office.

"I'm bleeding to death!"

"Are you sure?"

"YES, I am sure!"

"I'll be right there."

And he was. He pulled back my covers and saw me lying on the bedsheet, red up to my shoulders. "You're shaking."

"Call an ambulance—hurry up!"

He called an ambulance. Then he just stood there, wordless. Looking at me.

But he seemed to need to say something, anything. "What can I get you?"

"I am so cold!"

He piled the blankets from the foot of my bed on top of me, then the blankets from his bed.

He did not say, "Don't die, please don't die!"

He did not hold my hand.

As they carried me off on a gurney, I looked at Len and said, "Well, you almost got your chance to get rid of me."

He grimaced horribly, clenched his hands.

After the hysterectomy, I was left with a vertical scar about seven inches long. The scar soon spread out sideways until it was an ugly line, shiny like a burn, about an inch wide. Little dots, like the eyelets on a shoe, ran up by each side of the scar, where the surgeon had laced my wound shut.

Absolutely everything dug out and thrown away.

It was just about then that our wonderful young president was assassinated. The whole world mourned. People cried in public. I cried for him too. But I was still, in private, rejoicing for my own personal good fortune, at being rid of my female burden.

9

I made a point never to tell the girls what they should do when they got to Stanford. Yes, either of them could become a famous writer, or an archaeologist. But since neither of them wanted to be a doctor, they needed husbands to support them when they graduated. Everyone I knew assumed that almost all girls went to college to get married. That was the meaning of success.

The spring of her sophomore year, Jane began mentioning in her letters home a young man named Jack. She said he was handsome, had lots of friends, but was serious. They'd met in a Shakespeare class. They had coffee dates together, and soon they were having study dates in the evenings, in one of the little reading rooms at the student union.

He was a perfect gentleman to her, she reported demurely and with quiet pride.

Jack had been a debutante escort. Jane explained to us, like children, that it was the equivalent of a young woman being a debutante. His father was a lawyer, and they lived in southern California and had a second home at Lake Tahoe. Jack wanted to be a lawyer too.

He was pleased with Jane's art, which she would show him when he visited in the living room of her dormitory, Lagunita Hall. She gave him a still-life watercolor she'd made of a bowl of fruit. To thank her, he took her to the L'Alouette, the French restaurant on El Camino Real.

All went well, and stayed well.

Jane spent the summer at the ranch, riding her horse, pressing and sending wild flowers to her Jack. She wrote him a letter every third day. He wrote as often, the envelope addressed in blue fountain ink, with nice (but masculine) handwriting.

In the fall, back at school, Jane took advanced art studio classes. The human models embarrassed her terribly, but she kept at it. She shopped at Joseph Magnin for shirtwaist dresses. She made friends with other girls in her dorm who had serious boyfriends. Jack and Jane got season tickets to the San Francisco Symphony.

Jane mentioned her schoolwork less, and seemed entirely happy.

Jack came to Denver to meet us just after Christmas of their junior year. He was on his way to visit relatives in Chicago.

His plane arrived in midmorning. Jane, in a pastel shirtwaist and her tiny pearl earrings, went to pick him up. She was wearing her star sapphire ring from high school on her left hand. Such wishfulness.

And then there he was.

MY MOTHER'S AUTOBIOGRAPHY

Jack was six feet tall, beanpole thin and baby faced. Pale and black haired—Irish by his last name, which was good enough, in fact, fine!—like the Kennedys. And he was in a suit.

The three of us stepped in from the front door, and Len and Leah appeared.

Jane was embarrassed by Leah's giggling and impulsive hug. It was well into Leah's second year at Stanford, but apparently Jane had never introduced her eccentric sister to Jack.

Jane smiled up at her father. Len, in suit trousers and a white shirt and tie, welcomed the young man to our house. The young man said, "It's a pleasure to meet you, sir. Jane's always talking about her father. It's a pleasure to meet you."

Then somehow —almost immediately—Len said that he was the owner of the Mile-High Washing Machine Rental, the same grin on his face as when he'd boasted of his little riches to Virginia Gunderson.

I added quickly, "Jane's father also has an important job at United Airlines."

"What do you do?" Jack asked.

"I'm a dispatcher," Len said.

"Well, that's a misleading title," I explained. "Len's really a weatherman. He gives pilots information about weather on their routes."

Len added, "I do the Denver-to-Chicago route. That's where you're going, isn't it? I hope you're flying United."

I realized we were all standing in a close circle around the young man, bending forward, and he'd barely stepped through the front door, suitcase leaning against his leg.

"You must want to freshen up after your flight, and put your suitcase in your room," I said, and showed him to the bedroom in the basement, next to the furnace room. We'd fixed it up just for him, even gotten a new bed and a little chest of drawers.

That afternoon Jack and Jane sat on the sofa in the living room and listened to my three-record set of *Best Loved Classical Music*. They played a game of "Guess the Composer" with each other. The pair weren't even holding hands. They were like half-formed embryos of adulthood courting each other. I wondered if that was because Jane was so, well … moral.

I brought then a snack of red Jell-O and cookies. Jane pursed her lips when she saw the Jell-O.

We had my Sunday roast for dinner. I left out the onions, because not everybody likes them. I used my silver-plate gravy boat, the new wooden salad bowls, and my sateen table napkins. I wore my nice tan dress. After dinner, the five of us walked around the block, Jane and her young man in the rear, talking quietly. We had coffee when we got back to the house.

He flew on to Chicago the next afternoon.

Everything had gone so well. Would he propose in the spring?

Jack was apparently a very good student. He returned to California to tie up loose ends, and then he was off to study at Stanford's prestigious undergraduate campus in France. He asked Jane to wait past the winter and spring quarters for him; he would come back to her in the summer.

Jane did as she was asked. There was quiet pride in her voice when she called us on Sundays. She had so much to hope for now. It seemed they corresponded happily during winter term, and Jane continued to study art. But after fitful writing in April, Jack sent her nothing for two weeks. He sent her a long letter in May.

That evening, Jane called home. Her voice was tired. She had a bad cold, and she was coughing. She asked to talk to both of us. Len came in from the garage.

Jack had fallen in love with a girl at the campus in France and intended to marry her. In the letter he had begged Jane's forgiveness, and thanked her for the memories she'd given him.

Jane was terse, quietly panicked. Then, utterly alone and confused, she asked about her mare. "Are you sure she's all right? I miss her every day. The horses at the Stanford stable aren't nearly as fine as my horse. Not even the Lipizzaner. Nobody has a full-blooded, five-gaited, American Saddlebred like I do. She'd be the best horse there. I could ride her every day. The instructors and the trailers would be silent as we rode by."

Oh no.

Jane, the one who was always—even as a baby—beautiful as a movie star, pushed aside for a girl who couldn't possibly have been as pretty. She must have come from a rich, southern California family. Perhaps her father was a doctor or the president of a big corporation.

Jack, the unknown rich girl at the campus in France, Virginia Gunderson: peas in a rotten pod.

Putting the second phone down, Len came and stared at me with his mouth open, as though young people's whims had no right to destroy his dreams of moving upward.

Jane finished her classes, took her exams, stored her belongings in her trunk, and came home for the summer.

Oddly, Jane showed me the letter when she got here. At that moment in her life, I was all she had for a mother, wasn't I? As I read, she sobbed to herself, chin tucked in.

I told her he'd abandoned her, and that it was good riddance. Would she really want to marry someone capable of a trick like that? "And begging your forgiveness—he just had a guilty conscience. He just wanted to be left off the hook."

She listened without any reaction that I could tell. I touched her arm and she pulled away.

Jane and Leah rode and rode that summer, which was good, because it turned out that was the last summer of horses.

In the fall, after they'd gone back to Stanford, I convinced Len to sell the house on Bellaire Street. "Jack's leaving was all the fault of this run-down old bungalow, giving such a bad impression of us."

"There's nothing wrong with this house. You've fixed it up swanky, especially the living room. Not everyone has a blue carpet, blue drapes, a blue sofa. It's nice, period. If that boy didn't like it, there's something wrong with him."

"But Len, he had to sleep in the basement. He probably heard the furnace all night."

"This house is all paid off. My money goes to buying washing machines and dryers, and to paying the girls' Stanford tuition. Do you know how much that is? Do you hear me complaining about that?"

So I used my head. "How is Jane ever going to attract a husband we all can be proud of? And with a good, big house, we can all be proud of you."

We bought a pale-green ranch-style house with three bedrooms in a swanky neighborhood: Crestmoor Park.

"This makes us upper-middle class, doesn't it?" I said to Len after we moved in.

"Well, last year I made $100,000 with the Washing Machine Rental. That's what's talking."

10

Leah had always lived in a kind of foreign land somehow away from us, away from Denver and the ranch. It consequently wasn't surprising that she found a true home at Stanford. There she shined in English, Latin, Greek, and Italian. She even wedged in French and said that someday she was going to round it all out with Sanskrit. She got straight As. She was put in honors classes and still got straight As.

I breathed a sigh of relief. She had evolved far from that teenager who had sat immersed in strangeness and who had struck me in the face. At Stanford, she paraded to classes in a flashy, green plaid coat that billowed almost into a circle around her, and round steel glasses, the latest style, she said, among the students who were "intellectuals." She read *Lawrence of Arabia*. Leah was so enthusiastic about everything she encountered that she was almost embarrassing.

Len looked at Leah's first report card—four As and one A+. He solemnly said, "This is what we expect." Leah closed her eyes and breathed deeply at this, at her father oh-so-proud of her: Leah the star, not just the goldbricker.

In February, Jane called me one evening from the student union. She was shocked, almost whispering. "Leah wants to see a psychiatrist at the Student Health Center."

What? I dropped my crocheting down on the sofa.

Jane said she'd never known anyone who'd seen a psychiatrist. I whispered back, "Neither have I."

Len was sitting across from me in the living room, reading the newspaper. He'd noticed it was Jane I was talking to. "How are the girls doing?" he asked blandly when I hung up.

I told him both girls were *so* happy. I let that sink in. Then I said, "I miss the girls. Can I go see them, just for a day or two?" Len came over, got on the phone, and arranged a United pass for me, on the spot. He was obviously proud of himself, feeling prestigious—his eyes twinkled.

The following day, I flew out to San Francisco. Minutes into the flight, I saw we were over the front range of the mountains. I remembered Jane, and especially Leah, standing in our big meadow, waving up to the airplanes bound west. That was certainly a long time ago.

In Palo Alto, I got a room in a motel on El Camino Real.

All this to protect my child from herself.

Another mother would have brought a Bible with her to comfort her girl, reading Psalm 23 or some such thing. While I was packing, I'd thought of bringing my copy of Elizabeth Barrett Browning's *Sonnets from the Portuguese,* or Norman Vincent Peale's *The Power of Positive Thinking.* But the latter was full of Christianity. No, I had a better book—one that spoke in ageless truths. It was that Book of the Month Club selection, *The Prophet* by Kalil Gibran, a little foreign, but not too religious.

Jane and Leah arrived after dinner at their dorm. Leah was sallow in her green circle coat, and she had circles under her eyes. She hugged me without feeling and then folded up on the big bed. Jane wore her camel-hair jacket, and perched on the edge of the bed like she really didn't want to be there. I sat in the flower-print chair.

"Jane has told me you want to see a psychiatrist," I said.

Leah lay there.

I cocked my head. "*Why* do you want to see a psychiatrist?"

"I can't say. I can't put it in words," Leah said, looking at her feet.

"Everyone knows that will follow you for the rest of your life. You can be sure that Stanford will put that on your record, that you've seen a psychiatrist. They'll tell your professors.... Has someone said something to upset you?"

She didn't answer.

"Has someone?"

"No."

"Then what is it?"

"I just don't want to go home again."

"So where do you want to go then?"

"I don't know. But away." Leah lay there and shivered, then looked beyond me with flashing eyes. Like the times she'd crouched in the corner of her room, back home.

I saw she was trapped. Well, I was trapped too. So was Jane. We weren't just there in a motel room at night; we were in a foreign land, away from everything we knew. A land controlled by whatever was back behind those unseeing eyes. And we all had so much to lose, including Jane, because there would be rumors. But Leah would be hurt the most.

"Jane, you've never known anyone who's seen a psychiatrist, have you?" I asked.

"No, I haven't.... and what if Father finds out?" Jane bit her lower lip.

Would everything be suddenly changed? I too closed my eyes and felt cold. And I was the one who'd have to live with Len's anger and shame.

"Well, I've brought my copy of *The Prophet*. I want to read from it," I announced.

I straightened myself on the chair and had the girls sit on the floor, one on each side of me, as if it was ten years before, and they were eight and nine. I began reading, passages about eternity, about truth.

When you are sorrowful look again in your heart, and you shall see that in truth you are weeping for that which has been your delight.

I couldn't put in my own words what that meant but it was comforting, written, after all, by someone smart enough to write a book.

And know that yesterday is but today's memory and tomorrow is today's dream.

Leah—where was she? It was as though she were not in the room, had not heard a thing. I looked at Jane. She was still angry.

When it got close to the nine o'clock curfew in their dorm, I said, "Are you going to be all right now, Leah?"

"Yes, Mother." She looked up, eyes glancing hard, almost suspiciously, beyond my shoulder.

"Are you sure?"

"Yes, Mother." She looked at Jane, who was calling the front desk for a cab.

"Here. Keep the book. Keep it and read it instead of doing what you were going to do."

I walked out to the lobby's front door with them. "Stand straight," I told Leah. I held my arms out, and she hugged me back, remote. Her sister just walked to the other side of the cab and got in. I hoped Jane was all right. I would have hated to be in her position.

That night, lying in that huge motel bed in the dark, I thought it through. I had known what to do. What any mother would have done, if her daughter had been a danger to herself, out there halfway across the country. I'd explained to Leah the consequences of what she wanted to do, and I'd given her that book—better help than any psychiatrist could give her, anyway.

Suddenly, I was scared again. Were we through with this or not? Psychiatry sounded almost evil. They would have taken her over.

No. I was not scared. I'd made my point about that clearly, and Leah was smart; she'd see the truth of my words.

I sat alone in the first-class section, like all airline personnel did. I loved to look out the window when I flew. This flight, there were so many mountains beneath the airplane. The number of trees covering them was infinite. When the plane got high, the trees looked slate blue. We owned the top of one of those mountains. Were there any little girls down there waving at my airplane?

I could never tell Len why I'd gone to Palo Alto.

There's some old horror movie in which southern California, or someplace like it, is invaded, and an all-American family—including one young son, one teenage daughter—is attacked. The daughter is raped by a band of the invaders. After she is found, the dazed, destroyed daughter says, "I'm sorry, Daddy."

In a way, that was the world we lived in; there was danger everywhere for innocent girls, and Daddy was the person you never let down.

Even when a beautiful, perky stewardess served me lunch (chicken à la king) I couldn't stop thinking of consequences. The consequences of what a stranger might do to us. I hated being in that state of mind.

I couldn't be specific about what Len would have done to me about the psychiatrist business. Or what he would have done to Leah. Of course, I wasn't afraid of him. If anything, he was afraid of me.

All right, I was afraid of him. At the least, he would say what a terrible job I'd done raising Leah, and call me stupid.

I didn't think Leah remembered the time her father beat her. But she was still afraid of her father, for reasons she didn't seem to know. Jane didn't fear her father so much as she was always trying to protect him from bad news. Who it was going to come from was not clear to me, possibly not even to her.

We all lived on a narrow rock ledge, afraid of and simultaneously angry at each other.

Two weeks later, Leah called Len and me, to say she'd been chosen to attend the Stanford campus in Florence. I knew nothing about Florence, but she said it was an honor, and I was impressed. She'd be gone a year, traveling after the program was over.

She never mentioned the evening I read from *The Prophet*. She seemed to have no recollection of being desperate, of wanting to see a psychiatrist. None at all. Had that trip of mine been a waste of time? No, no—the exact opposite. She'd been completely cured, surely, of whatever had been ailing her. Yes. I felt a moment of pride, and of intelligence.

Then Leah was gone. She sent back postcards from everywhere in Italy. Then Cairo, Jerusalem, Athens, Budapest, Paris, Munich, and even Moscow. I pictured her strewing foreign language rubies from her lips, and rubies tumbling from the now-conversant hands that, she wrote us, she'd learned to gesture with.

Fourteen months later, she was back in our home in Crestmoor Park, resplendent in her now-long black hair and big sunglasses. She'd sold the green plaid coat on the black market in Moscow; she had a tailored, rose-colored linen coat from Rome now. For other moods, she had a huge floppy hat—purple and red—"mini" skirts, "midi" dresses she'd bought in London, white boots, black boots. Dangling earrings. Her ancient Greek dictionary in a big leather bag from Rome.

And life was unfair to staunch, dignified Jane, in every way.

She graduated without marriage, just left Stanford. They had to mail her diploma to her. Her grades were low, and her degree in art history was, well, useless. So—with hesitation and seemingly unfocused vague resentments—she joined the Peace Corps in 1966, along with all the other young people without direction who didn't get into medical school, who were avoiding the draft and Vietnam.

Don't get me wrong; I knew there were other kinds in the Peace Corps too. A lot of the young people were dreamers, out to change every corner of the world for better. You could read about them in the newspapers, and see stories about them on TV.

Jane went into a distant world for two years. Letters took a long time between the United States and North Africa, a week, or two or three: all stale mail when they did arrive.

I had Jane and Leah's mares, now too old to sell, put out to pasture at the old man's place on the other side of the mountain. Len and I went up to the ranch less and less, mostly just to check up on things. It was as though fall was always in the air, even when it wasn't. There was that fall strangeness, as though things were dying, even though they weren't. I was confused, in a big-but-quiet way. I kept it to myself. Who would care? Who would understand? I wondered if I had a place in any of this at all.

11

It became Len's time to shine.

I never knew he wanted to be a leader. I knew he loved being a big shot, but being a leader? That didn't feel right to me. Even within his job at United Airlines, he worked mostly alone, him and his weather maps.

Then the supervisor's position fell open. Supervisor of the Denver dispatchers, a man who would work nine-to-five-thirty—not shifts. A supervisor had a secretary, and his own partitioned room.

Len had worked in his job for twenty years. Now he wanted that big honor.

He'd never had an honor, after all. But imagine it—being in management! He was even willing to leave the union, because either you're union or you're management. Of course, among the fifteen dispatchers in the office, others wanted that honor too.

Days, weeks—so many rumors—of slow excitement, all eyes turning to the door whenever management men came in the office. Could it be news, had they made their choice yet?

Len would come home from work each day of June 1966, full of rumors, hope, desire. He'd sit at the kitchen table, suggesting to me certain signals that meant certain things.

I would say, now, that those were the best weeks of our marriage. Even better than the year Jane was born and we were full of energy and dreams from BF Goodrich. Even better than the year we bought the ranch, with all that space and air and owning it. That summer of '66, he shared with me *in words* what he hoped.

He wanted it so badly.

And then one morning (he was working the midnight shift) he walked in the front door at 8:15, and sat down at the dinette table, still in his suit jacket. He sat straight up. For a minute, he didn't move. Then he slapped his hand down on the table,

"I got the job." He looked up at me with shining eyes.

That was the best moment of his life.

He was fifty-four years old.

I closed my eyes and pulled my bathrobe tight across my chest, and the moment poured over me too. A life new in every way—an adventure. And I would be a management wife.

I could see myself at the management Christmas party, sought out for my *opinions*. Standing tall, in a nice suit. Another manager, or even the Denver vice-president, might ask me what I thought about one thing or another. I could say to Len, "*We* work for United Airlines."

I looked back at him. I saw a glint of fear pass through his eyes. I felt it pass through me too.

Within the week, Len had bought a Mercury Cougar. I was happy for him. As he had with the Lincoln Continental years earlier, he brought it home paid for, a complete surprise to me. But this time, the fact that I owned the ranch, had it and all its monetary value in my own hands, somehow made up for that. Ownership is a baffling thing, and it brings unspoken rules.

Anyway, I admired his reasoning about the car's look. A brand-new Mercury sedan, purchased just for the occasion, would have perhaps seemed showy, certainly so to higher management. And a Mustang, so popular then, would have seemed too sporty for a man Len's age. He chose a pale-green Cougar. The greenness surprised me. It was almost delicate for someone who had so much of the working man in him. Or maybe he was trying to hide that.

When Leah came back at the end of the term, I asked her if her big burgundy purse was real leather.

"Of course it is. It's from Europe," she said, as though everyone should know that.

"You're always talking about being a lady, Mother. So why don't *you* have a leather purse?"

Leah went back, with all her stylishness, to Stanford summer school, and I drove down to Neusteters to get a real purse.

Purses and shoes were on the first floor. I looked all around and listened to the chatter of the smartly dressed ladies picking up purses from the displays, examining them, holding them beside their high heels to see if they matched.

So, they were supposed to match. All the years of mismatched purses and shoes, all through my life—I looked back and winced. But now I was the wife of an almost-rich man, a man who was also in management at United Airlines.

Well, I did know that in the summer a lady carries a white purse. So I chose a white patent-leather purse with a small, elegant handle fastened on with gold links. Smart. Then I walked across the aisle and almost immediately spotted a pair of matching shoes I liked. Small straps crisscrossed their open toes. The heels were only an inch high; I wouldn't totter.

The wife of a supervisor.

That summer we had each of the eight senior dispatchers, with their families, up to the ranch for a steak cookout on the patio—one family every Saturday.

The senior dispatchers were high-school educated, the lowest rung of the white-collar world. I'd come to a private conclusion, learning little things about them from Len across the years, that as a whole they were kind of cookie-cutter men, kind of bland.

Each couple arrived in the middle of the afternoon, the man in tan slacks and the wife in pedal pushers or a summer dress. Len had the tractor parked up by the cabin to give the husband a tour of the ranch, and I took the woman and the children (if they'd brought them) into my kitchen.

I'd put my white purse on the far end of the kitchen table, where I was sure they could see it. I wore a pale-green rayon dress, with open-toed patent-leather shoes, of course. Clear nail polish. I felt like a hostess.

The first women deferred to me like I was a military wife whose husband outranked hers. I kind of enjoyed that. In a way it was my due, after all was said and done about Len and all those years of him. A wife rose in the ranks, just as her husband did. "*We* are with United Airlines."

The fourth woman who visited put her purse down on my big kitchen table with its new yellow tablecloth to match the yellow walls. Hers was a tan vinyl purse, cracked in the seams, with two very long straps. "It must be nice to be able to afford a big place like this, up here in the mountains. Someday *we* hope to get a little cabin."

"Of course you will! United will be good to you, just as it's been good to Len and me."

"Yes, but my Mike's been at United almost as long as Len, and Mike is still working the midnight shift."

I wanted her to like me, but she didn't. All I felt from her was resentment. "Did you say your son has just graduated high school?" I asked. "You must be proud. What's he doing next?"

"We don't know. He hasn't got the grades, and we don't have the money for him to go to college."

"I'm sorry to hear that. But you're so lucky to have a son. All I had were girls."

"I've heard your girls are at Stanford University."

"Yes, we're very fortunate."

"You're fortunate you can afford it."

"Well, it's been hard, but we're careful."

I knew she didn't believe that, because she said, "What a chic patent-leather purse you have, Mrs. Hope."

It was sitting there, white and shiny.

"Thank you. I bought it on sale."

"I couldn't afford one like that, even on sale."

The tractor rolled up outside. She and I went out to meet the men.

"This is some tractor he's got here," Mike shouted over to his wife as he was getting off. "He'll always be able to get himself a job driving a tractor."

Len grinned. The dumb grin sat on his face as he built the fire in the patio pit and, flames snapping, gingerly placed the steaks on the grill over it.

I brought out the three-bean salad, sliced bread, and Jell-O. The wife didn't offer her help.

After dinner at the new picnic table, Len continued to smile as we all sat around the fire on patio chairs, while the sun set. He started up conversation. "This man, Mike here, is a hard worker, and the best map-reader in the office."

His wife said, "Yes, my Mike is a hard worker. So is our son. So am I."

"Well, Len works all the time," I said.

"What all do you do, Mrs. Hope?" the wife asked, uninterested.

"Oh, really, I don't work so very hard. I have a heart condition, you know." I hoped that bit of knowledge would win her over to me a little, somehow.

"Well, perhaps you shouldn't live so high up."

Len laughed. That had gone right over his head.

He was proud of that evening. Smile on his face—things were going well for him indeed. In every way.

When we got back down to Denver and I was alone again in the house, I thought of writing a note in bright-red lipstick on my mirror:

Do I exist?

MY MOTHER'S AUTOBIOGRAPHY

I wondered, with a little smile to myself, what Len would make of that. Since I didn't immediately know the answer to either question, I went and got a piece of The Mile-High Washing Machine Rental business stationary and wrote:

I exist to Len as a steady irritant who burdened him with a family. I exist to Jane as the unladylike mother who has never met any of her needs. I exist to Leah as someone who makes her angry each time I open my mouth.

I exist as Anne Elizabeth. But that's just the name my parents gave me.

I have brown eyes, an ugly face, and a body that's often a nuisance and a burden to me and to others. But all that's just inherited.

I supervise, cook, clean, drive. But that's what I do, not what I am.

I know I exist when I squish my toes around in the warm, soapy water in my little plastic tub, prior to bending down and cutting my nails.

I know I exist when I make a little joke and nobody else gets it, but I know it's funny.

when I think back to Claire, and know I had a true friend.

when I recall a little log house out there in the woods, that I never told any of them about.

when I allow that I'm smart, regardless of his calling me stupid and the girls mindlessly agreeing.

I know I exist just as I know God does not.

I know I exist when I remind myself this is

not the life I would have wanted.
I know I exist when I feel alone in the world.
When I was done, I folded the note up and put it in the bottom of my jewelry box.

12

I wouldn't have said Len wasn't intelligent back in those days. Maybe he was, and I just never figured it out. He could understand any machine, and he could dream big— the same dream for years on end. Those were signs of intelligence. But as far as people were concerned, he was just unaware, completely unaware. He seemed to have one meter: whether people thought he was a big shot. If they didn't, like Virginia, he could come to, well, almost hate them. Almost.

The men in his office, whatever their self-serving or resentful or good-natured or hard-working motivations, did what he asked them to do. And he basked in that. He was a manager of men.

By the end of the summertime steak cookouts for those men, another thing had happened which caused Len to bask even more. He'd found a friend indeed in Charles Thatcher, who, with his wife Alice, had moved in next door to our house in Denver, in elegant Crestmoor Park.

It was funny; Alice and I met on a September morning at our incinerators, at the far ends of our backyards, beside the alley. I was taking out the burnable trash from my kitchen, and so was she from hers.

Len and I knew we had new neighbors, because we'd seen the moving van, the two new cars now parking in the garage next door, and then a pair of large yellow Labrador puppies romping in their yard, playing fetch with yellow tennis balls thrown by a handsome middle-aged man.

Alice was small and had short tan hair, in her early fifties, like me. She was pretty. She stood with me in the warm morning sun there in our backyards while the puppies tore around her yard with her emptied brown grocery bag. "What a lovely, brisk day … I hear it's going to get windy this afternoon," she said.

"Yes," I replied. "Soon it's going to be full fall. Our young oak tree there—and yours—will be bright red. Won't that be beautiful!"

We took to talking. She'd been a librarian once, before she'd married her husband, Charles, the man who'd played with the dogs the afternoon before. She said she didn't miss it at all; there were still so many books to read.

Alice and Charles had just moved stateside, as she put it, after years of assignment with their oil company in Indonesia. "We liked it there, the Brits and the Americans were friendly and warm, but the people of Jakarta were so poor. I always felt so sorry for them."

That made me like her.

I suddenly thought back to Virginia. She had never felt sorry for anyone except herself, when she'd coated her kitchen walls with soup from an exploded pressure cooker. Alice, on the other hand, was a woman who read books, who was a housewife in a house like mine. She would not envy my beautiful purse, or my steaks on a patio in the mountains. She was fundamentally like me.

"I have two daughters and a son," Alice said when I invited her afterward to my dinette for midmorning coffee. "Our son has decided on petroleum engineering, like Charles. Two peas in a pod. My one daughter, Peggy, is married and has a one-year-old boy. My other daughter, Susan, is nineteen. She's, well, 'finding herself.' You know how they do, at that age."

"Oh yes, I know. My older daughter is finding herself in the Peace Corps right now."

Alice and I were both wearing our daughters' cast-off t-shirts. Mine said "Stanford University," and hers said "The Beatles." I pointed that fact out, and we both laughed.

"And you have another child?" Alice asked.

"Oh yes, it's her last year at Stanford. Quite the success at learning languages. And Len works for United Airlines."

"Is he a pilot?"

"Oh, no. He's a manager in Flight Operations." I left out the word "dispatcher" because I knew enough to know that in her circle "dispatcher" would sound like someone who works for Yellow Cab. "But you have a grandchild—lucky you."

We exchanged a happy smile.

As I said, Charles and Len hit it off too. That was apparent the first time the Thatchers had us over for cocktails. Charles was a he-man, tall with straight, heavy blond hair and a rugged jaw, born—as was Alice—in Wyoming.

I was in awe of their living room. A hand-painted Japanese screen, two Japanese dolls in glass cases, a statue of a Siamese goddess, a wall collection of blue-and-white china that had been added from faraway assignments and traveling abroad. What a wonderful life they'd led! Alice handed me a gift when we sat down: a yellow-and-blue tie-dyed tablecloth for my dinette. "It's folk art from Indonesia," she said.

I put my hand to my mouth and almost gasped. "Oh, Alice, those are my favorite colors." And they were, too.

The two men had scotch. Alice and I had sherry. I'd learned to sip it in the aftermath of Virginia. Suddenly, I felt sorry for that woman and her excesses. Then she was gone from my thoughts.

The men spoke of their busy offices, of overseeing other men, even of their secretaries.

Of their lands—our ranch and Charles' ranch in Wyoming—Charles said, "We'll probably retire there someday. You'll have to come visit us then."

They spoke of their children, each surely headed in some interesting direction toward success. They especially spoke of the Thatcher son.

As the scotch made Len jovial, he put his chin in the air and smiled that puckered-lipped, self-satisfied smile I disliked.

But I *was* glad for him. Glad he had someone to exchange that particular smile with. I tried to think back to a time when … no, it had never happened before. Here was respect. Yes, I was glad for him. And when had *I* ever been respected before? It was, in all its seeming tininess, a monumental moment for both of us.

"It's good to have good neighbors," Charles laughed forcefully. Len caught my eye.

He caught my eye.

We got together again, then again soon after that. Charles never mentioned Len's lack of education. Len never mentioned being, almost all his life, a union man. But now, after all, he was in management among Republicans like Charles. Len kind of went out of his way not to appear around Crestmoor Park in his overalls.

Of course, none of this was ever put into words.

That fall, we took to having cocktails together on Fridays, as soon as the men came home from work. We alternated between their house and ours.

Something was happening inside of Len. It was the logical result, I could see, of his new job and of his friendship with Charles. Len was starting to hide the Mile-High Washing Machine Rental. And to think—it had been his dream, the big dream of his life, for nearly twenty years. He'd knocked on the doors of apartment managers to get their business, over and over through the years, fixed broken washers and dryers in apartment basements, at night, during the day, weekdays and weekends—really, whenever he could be off shift, never mind the weather—always alone. Across the years, down in those basements, he'd collected dimes and quarters from the machines' coin boxes, driving down dark alleys as he collected his coins, heavy bags by the end, which he'd sort, in the early years by hand, later with a metallic contraption. Then he'd go to the bank once a month, a proud man with the fruits of his labors. It had been his everything. He'd boasted of it to Virginia, and then to Jane's rich boyfriend. He'd come to hate them both for turning aside.

Now, when we had cocktails with Charles and Alice, I never seemed to catch him mentioning the Mile-High Washing Machine Rental. I didn't know what was going through his head, what he was sorting out, or how. We didn't talk about it. It was his own dream.

One Friday during cocktails, a few months into our friendship, Len said to Charles: "I meant to tell you—I have a little business on the side. Appliances. I have two employees."

That's as far as his near-secret, the little dream company, went. Not just because it was workmen's work, but because Len was a solitary man. A solitude no one could enter—not me anyway, and probably not Charles.

Sometimes I wished Jane were back, so she could talk with him; if in fact the two of them did talk. Perhaps they just kept silence together. In a way, I knew Jane better than I knew Len. For her, dignity forbade telling the innermost parts of oneself. For Len … I never did know what kept Len to himself. But I imagined Jane missed him terribly, over there.

Meanwhile, Leah was searching around for new, adventurous things to do, or so it seemed. Jane had never much liked Leah's eccentricities, and Leah had needed that always-present slight disapproval to help keep her in line. Now that Jane was gone, Leah seemed to do whatever moved her fancy.

What moved her fancy now was her French. When she came back to Denver in December, she spent the whole of Christmas vacation in her bedroom, listening to monotonous-sounding phrases on her tape recorder and reciting French verbs out loud to herself. She sat on her carpeted floor, the snow coming down outside her windows, amid little stacks of flash cards whose various groupings had meaning to her. One day I pointed out the snow on the ground outside, the big flakes falling, and she said, "I don't care. I'm warm." That was it.

She did not leave her room. Len was mad that he'd bothered to get her an airplane ticket to come home for Christmas. I decided not to put up a tree; I couldn't see the point of it. In a way, it was my first Christmas as an "empty-nester." I felt, some moments, completely alone. I wondered if that feeling would just fade across time until I felt nearly nothing, until I just went through the day.

Jane sent us a Christmas card with an embossed Moslem angel. That card was our Christmas with Jane. We all wrote her letters, of course. But we couldn't send packages; Jane had said they'd too likely be lost or stolen in the mail over there. We couldn't call her; she had no phone. And, she wrote, certainly no one at the central phone station there could speak enough English to connect her with the States anyway.

She likely couldn't bake a ham or a turkey in her primitive kitchen. They probably didn't have hams or turkeys in North Africa. So, Jane slipped a little further away from our immediate thoughts.

Alice was over for midmorning coffee with me. The Thatchers' Christmas was turning out to be a mosaic of comings and goings. Peggy (the older sister), her husband, and the baby came for two days while on their way to Florida. A warm—even hot—Christmas awaited them there, with her husband's parents. Alice and Charles' son stopped by on his way to assignment in Louisiana. Both of them were happy that he would not, after all, be going to work overseas.

"And Susan will not be coming home this year," Alice said, her eyes on her coffee cup. She picked up her spoon, thought something over, and put the spoon back down. "Susan is our Wednesday's Child, full of woe."

I impulsively reached to touch Alice's wrist.

"She can't seem to settle, to alight on anything." Alice laughed nervously, but she was far away from me, in her own thoughts. "I imagine Susan's wings get pretty tired and sore, hovering like that."

Alice looked up and raised her eyebrows. She took a long breath. "Susan can't make up her mind about anything. She's nineteen, and she's lost. Last summer, she worked on a dude ranch. But she quit halfway through the summer. Right now she's up in Boulder, selling jewelry to students in a shop close to campus. We don't know how long that will last."

A lost daughter. How on earth would she handle that? Oddly, Jane came to my mind just then. I'd hit on a perfect solution to get her through the unfocused, resentful stage: the Peace Corps. But Alice's daughter was too young for that, and a dropout. My Jane was *not* a dropout. She always finished what she started. And so much of what had happened to her hadn't been her fault, after all. I could even say I was proud of Jane.

"Susan has no friends. She's never had a date. She doesn't read. Anne, it hurts me to say this, but she's so very lost that we've asked her to see, well, a professional, if you know what I mean." Alice paused. "But we don't think she will."

The pity I felt—to have a daughter with that kind of problem. I closed my eyes and saw, against the brilliant redness inside my eyelids, Leah's face as I read to her from *The Prophet* in that hotel room in California. She'd been cured immediately of what had been eating at her. Yes, I was proud of what I'd done. But I could never tell Alice—not even Alice—about that brush with the taboo "professional."

Instead I said, "Oh, Alice, I'm so very sorry for you. And the tragedy of it is that you're such a brave mother, such a good mother."

13

Leah graduated in June of 1967. I told Len what Phi Beta Kappa was and showed him how it was spelled.

"So that was money well invested," he said.

Then my younger daughter packed up her posters, clothes, and books, left her dorm, and was almost on her own. She seemed to see nothing odd about renting some professor's attic in Atherton, a super-rich suburb near Stanford, and spending the summer reviewing Latin, Greek, Italian, and French grammar books and flashcards. And now she had Italian tapes as well as the French ones. She wrote us that she spent an hour on each language in the mornings, took the afternoon off to have lunch at the student union and then "hang out," as she put it, on campus. Then she'd go back to her "Parisian artist's garret" to do four more hours of languages in the evening.

Len didn't mind paying Leah's small rent for the summer, in view of the fact that she'd been given a large fellowship for the following school year, and after that would almost certainly be on her own financially.

"Len, she must have five-thousand flash cards that she just goes over and over and over."

"Well, at least we know where she is," he said.

14

In those days, Len's life at United Airlines was completely filled up with his boss, Johnny Scannell, the next man up in Flight Operations.

"He acts like he owns my boys," Len complained. "He goes right up to their desks and talks to them before he even says hello to me." He took a deep, sharp breath. "He comes into *my* office unannounced, arrogant bastard."

Len was proud of his personal office, the first room to the right as you entered the dispatchers' station. Nobody else there had a private room. It was an extended, wooden cubicle with a table and typing chair for his secretary, a chair for a visitor, and his own large desk and chair. I visited it once. I remarked that there were no pictures on the walls, no photo of me or the girls or the ranch on his desk.

"Well, you get me some, and I'll have Evelyn put them up," he replied. "Anyway, there's Evelyn's picture of her husband beside her typewriter." It was kind of like his not wearing a wedding ring, really. The same sort of—what, sexlessness? No, I shouldn't have thought that. Women who were feminine didn't think like that. Maybe Leah would, but *I* wouldn't.

Anyway, Len kept his door open. He prided himself on being that kind of a boss.

"Johnny doesn't knock. He doesn't even rap on the wall before coming in. Today I went to the toilet, and when I came back, Johnny was in my office, having a big old conversation with Evelyn. I had to go back to my chair and sit there and wait on him until he stopped talking with her."

I would have been mad too. Anyone would have been.

One day I asked Len to describe Johnny Scannell to me. "Well …" he couldn't find words. Then he said angrily, "He's fat. He needs to do real man's work, you know, work with his hands. That's what he needs. Otherwise, one of these days he's going to have a heart attack. Which would be no skin off my back."

Johnny had asked him to write a report about how the dispatch office worked, from Len on down. Who reported to who, who made what decisions, how they interacted with the other dispatch offices (especially Chicago and San Francisco), and protocols with the pilots and with the larger Flight Operations.

"That Johnny Scannell took one look at me and didn't like me. He just wants to replace me, and he's going to make it easy for someone else to step in. That's what this goddamn report is really about."

But Len couldn't write well at all. The once-a-month letters he wrote Jane, exactly two pages long, depleted him. He didn't have the slightest idea how to do this report for Scannell.

However, I did. I'd typed report after report at BF Goodrich when I was young and working. I knew never to use the word "I." And I knew how to make an outline, one that included *I, II, A, B, a, b,* and so forth.

So, over a period of two weeks, I wrote up the report of his office for him, and then typed it up on the Mile-High Washing Machine Rental typewriter down in the basement. My report had perfect margins on the top, sides, and bottom, as well as perfect indentations. I told him to give it to Evelyn to retype with her initials, and to make mimeographed copies—including one for me.

I saved the day for my husband. And I can't say he wasn't grateful. He didn't bring me flowers, and he didn't take me out to dinner. But predictably, he mussed up my hair with his hand and swiped his lips over the part on its side and said, "I guess I owe you one, Anne."

"Yes, STUPID me," I replied, pulling my head away.

"Well, I do owe you one."

"Yes, in fact you do."

He raised his eyebrows at my even, steady voice.

"Alice Thatcher's husband gave her ten-thousand dollars, so she could have some money that was her very own," I said.

Len looked stunned. The skin of his cheeks pulled back defensively. "I won't give you ten-thousand, and you damn well know it."

"I want five-thousand."

"Isn't it enough that you own the ranch? That you could sell it right out from under me and there's not one damn thing I could do about it?"

"Okay, big boy, I'll call Evelyn and tell her just who wrote that report, and maybe the word will get back to Johnny Scannell."

Len hit his thigh with the palm of his hand. It made a big, angry smack. He screwed his face up with that ugly grimace of his that meant defeat.

"All right. Go open up a credit union account in your name, and I'll write you a check for five-thousand dollars."

I caught his eye and carefully licked my upper lip with the tip of my tongue.

I smiled at him, and—the oddest thing ever—he smiled back as he walked away.

15

Jane had been gone for well over a year. There was still no way to call her in North Africa, and no way for her to develop photographs and send them to us. She was so far away, on the edge of the Sahara. Maybe because she felt lonely, she went and got herself that boyfriend. I wondered from the beginning what more we could have done. I wrote her twice every week. I'd write her about her childhood cat, which was now so old that he lived almost entirely in sleep. I sent her photographs of him, and photographs of the rest of us. Len wrote her on the first day of each month. He took it as a solemn duty.

When Jane replied, she wrote nothing personal, just about the Peace Corps, the local customs, the seasons. Just descriptions. How the Arab housewives had to dust and dust because of the fine sand which the winds brought in from the Sahara all day, every day. About the young girls in the English class she taught, who at first didn't want to take their veils off—even in the privacy of her classroom—and how one day or another, a girl would be missing from class, never to return; she had been married off to someone by her parents. The water-carriers on the streets, with their brass bowls. The men who sat cross-legged with flutelike pipes and enticed big snakes out from their straw baskets, to sway to haunting melodies in front of small crowds on the edge of the souks. The souks so intricate they hadn't been mapped by the French colonists until the end of the nineteenth century. Every day so hot, so very hot—until winter came and with it the horses' suffering. The horses became so thin, really skin and bones, the dying ones with their tongues hanging down, driven to their very end by the Arabs to get the last bit of work out of them, pulling carriages, carts, wagons. How it hurt Jane to see the horses suffer. That was the only letter in which she let her own self show.

    I wondered if she still wore her hair long. How did American girls dress over there?

    It felt like Jane was keeping us at arm's length, from half a world away. It never occurred to me that she had a secret.

    But she did, and his name was Alan Wong.

    I read that letter, and when I got to the word "Chinese," I— I could not say. I could not put it into words that anyone would understand. I was not prejudiced. I had *The Family of Man* on my coffee table. I had taken the girls to hear Martin Luther King. I had never been a prejudiced person and never would be. I raised them saying, "You can't hate a person for the color of his skin." Alan (and Jane) could not accuse me of that.

    Besides, he hated me long before he met me. She hated me because she just up and presumed I'd be prejudiced against him, along with all the other walls she'd constructed against me: resentment at my pointing out that her grades at Stanford weren't as high as she was capable of.

Well, she did give up easily, and that was a fact. And her deciding I was cruel to her father! Once she looked me in the eye and said, "The trouble with you, Mother, is that you're snide."

But someone from another *race*? That was wrong, so fundamentally wrong. The entire world knew you weren't supposed to mix the races. Did they hold hands? Did they hold hands in public, for all to see? Did they actually kiss? I shrank from the image. What if they had children? The children would look strange. Would people exchange glances as children, neither white nor yellow, passed by? I was—yes—frightened. I took a deep breath; perhaps someday I would have to shake hands with him.

Len came home that day from the dispatch office with anger in his eyes. He swept through the kitchen, pulled out the nearest dinette chair and sat, still in his suit jacket. He raised his outstretched hand, presumably to complain about his day, and began, "Boy, let me tell you what that man pulled today—"

I turned away.

"Anne, are you listening to me?"

I walked up to his face. "Len, you listen to me. Jane wrote us today that she has a boyfriend now—a Chinese boy!"

He lowered his head, and his eyes focused hard on the floor. Then he closed his eyes just as hard, and took a deep breath. He looked like a dumb ox in a yoke. Or a North African horse that had been driven as far as it could go.

"Well, you'll just have to put a stop to that. That can't go on."

"Just what the hell do you mean? You are her *father*. You are the head of this house."

"I am not every goddamn thing everybody wants me to be. Johnny Scannell *this*, you *that*, those two selfish, spoiled girls … you write that girl and tell her to come to her senses. Right now I have to put on my overalls and go fix a goddamn washer."

"You could have one of your men do it."

"I want to get the hell away from everyone." He stood there and fumed. "I am being pulled in every goddamn direction."

"Len …"

"I'll get a hamburger somewhere on the road."

What if she got pregnant on the other side of the world?

The next morning, alone, I went about my business. It was my day to vacuum and dust. Dusting made me think of those poor Arab women with all that sand from the Sahara. As I lifted each of my paltry vases and figurines, I thought, *What if our families found out about Alan Wong? What if Johnny Scannell found out? What if anyone found out?* I could never tell anyone. I'd never felt so alone in my life.

They were young. It could fizzle. Maybe she wouldn't come home with him. What if she did?

Everyone who knew us would conclude what a bad mother I was, raising her like that: rejecting her. But it wasn't my fault Jane never listened to me about those things from the time she was a teenager. The fact is, she'd done this before. Was I *really* supposed to let her go to the East High senior prom with a Miguel Padilllo? I'd heard from another mother that he even had an accent. Jane did not understand that I was protecting her reputation, her future—like a mother bear protecting her cubs.

I could still see her face the moment I told her she had to break that date; she rejected me permanently, her eyebrows raised, her lips pursed into a little hole in her beautiful face.

This time I had no one on my side, not even Len saying automatically, "Obey your mother."

Len didn't ask if I'd written her. Well, I hadn't.

Jane's old yellow cat was dying. He was spending a long time dying of old age, days and nights, lying there on my black-and-purple crocheted afghan, which I always kept on the sofa. Friday, the fourth morning after Jane's letter arrived, I got up after Len had gone to the office. I started the coffee and went to the living room to look at the weather through the picture window. A gray autumn day presented itself to me. I turned back and saw that Jane's cat was no longer breathing. It had happened, without her. Sorrow for Jane, sorrow about her, just sorrow to mingle with all the grayness of the day itself—I wanted none of this to have happened, and it all had. I went to gather her cat up in my arms. He was already stiff. I put him in a brown grocery bag and placed it in the garage, by the kitchen door. Len could bury him when he got home that evening, after we came back from the Thatchers'. Then I was glad it was over.

I fixed myself two pieces of toast and sat down at the dinette table and began to write Jane.

"I'm going to get my hair colored tomorrow," I told Alice later that morning. I'd invited her over for coffee.

"I like the way it is now. That little streak of gray emphasizes your high forehead. It's lovely, Anne."

"I don't know. I need something new. For October, for when the leaves turn. Just something new."

"The leaves will turn yellow, red. Ask your hairdresser for auburn."

Auburn. My hair then so elegant.

I'd invited her over to show her my daughter's letter about the boyfriend. I had to show it to someone. To Alice. I wondered if Alice and Charles had oriental house boys when they lived in Indonesia. Houseboys.

I couldn't use the word Jane had used. I couldn't even mouth it. But if I passed Jane's letter to Alice, she could read the word. If the word was going to be said, Alice could say it. Suddenly, I felt tired from everything.

"Are you all right, Anne?" Alice asked, bending forward.

My lips trembled. Alice extended her hand over mine.

"We've had some news," I said. "Some very bad news. From North Africa." I let my head fall.

"Anne ... I'm so sorry.... What can I do?"

I turned, took the fragile airmail letter from the counter, and handed it to Alice. I clenched my eyes shut.

"Anne, do you want me to read it?"

"Yes, Alice. Please read it. Thank you."

My eyes filled with tears. I pushed back my chair, stood, and went to the living room. I sat on the sofa, beside the black-and-purple afghan, and wiped my eyes with a tissue.

I waited. *Alice must be reading the letter twice*, I thought. I stared through the picture window at the young oak's leaves, which were turning shades of auburn. But the sky was still gray, and the grass in the backyard was losing its greenness. *Becoming gray like the sky.*

I felt Alice's presence beside me.

"May I sit on your lovely afghan, Anne?" she whispered.

"Oh, but it's covered with cat hairs. Jane's old cat died on it last night. I haven't had a chance to shake it out." I put my hand over the afghan, without knowing why.

"I'm so sorry ..."

"It was almost like the last bit of Jane. We got him for her when she was a little girl, and now the cat's gone too."

"What was the cat's name?"

"Dearest."

"She called him 'Dearest'?"

"Yes. She would call him in at night before she went to bed. She'd call 'Dearest, Dearest!' into the dark. Sometimes Len would help her call her cat home. He'd be out in the backyard with her, both of them calling, 'Dearest, Dearest ...'"

I clenched my hands and said loudly, "Such a stupid name. Almost as stupid as the Peace Corps. And all those dirt-poor countries starving their horses and cats. And all the young American women over there," I added, with a sob that surprised me completely.

I began to cry. Bent over, I cried for a long time. I wrung my hands. Alice rubbed my back with the palm of her hand as she bent toward me. I made my face wet, and my hands, and the front of my blouse.

"It's all right, Anne. All will be well. Trust me, all will be well. She must love him a great deal."

I heard Len's car drive up in front of the garage. He must have come home for lunch. He rarely did that. I hoped he hadn't brought anger from his office back with him. I dried my tears and blew my nose. Alice excused herself and went home.

Len came in the living room and looked at me. His face turned tender. I stared at that.

"I just came home to tell you I got up a little after midnight last night to use the toilet. I went out and checked on Dearest. I held him while he died. I just wanted you to know," he said. There was a tiny bit of pride in his voice.

"*You* did that?"

That hurt him. I added quickly, "That was very kind of you, Len. I'll tell Jane when she comes home."

"Well," he said, "get me some lunch, will you?"

16

In early December, Charles and Alice went up to the Thatcher family ranch in Wyoming and returned with a modest load of pine wood in the back of their station wagon. So, we had two evenings' worth of fire in their fireplace and two in ours.

A few days passed after the wood was used up, and then Alice said, "You know, I miss the coziness of a pine fire."

Len's face brightened. "I've got a truck with a large bed. Let's drive up to our ranch for the day sometime soon and get a real load of wood. I've already got about two cords cut up for the winter, stacked right in front of the cabin, on the patio. We can load up some of that."

"Then we could see your ranch," Alice said. "Anne and I could walk around while you two are working."

"I'd love to show you my woods behind the cabin," I answered her. "It's very special to me. I've never shown it to anybody else."

"No, I've got a better idea," Charles said. "Alice and Anne can stay home, maybe have a nice lunch over in Cherry Creek and then go to the library together. Len and I can he-man it together up there over the weekend."

"Now you're talking. I'll take you for a tour of the place on my big tractor." Len grinned. I was thrilled for him. "We can get out there and do real work," he added. "We'll take a bottle of Johnny Walker and some beer, and Anne and Alice can make us sandwiches, maybe even some ham."

The plans moved fast. They left the next Friday after work in Len's now-old, baby-blue truck and planned to come back Sunday afternoon, the bed of the truck piled high with wood, Len in overalls and Charles in blue jeans, both with plaid wool shirts. Charles sported a cowboy hat.

They called me and then Alice when they got to the cabin and, much later, as they were getting ready for bed. "That Charles is a real character," Len said then, seemingly giving the other man a glance as he gushed, voice liquored. He sounded so happy, man-to-man—the first time in his life, since the rubber pits?

He called me after lunch on Saturday. Weather was coming in, he said. "But we'll be fine. We'll just get an early start tomorrow, if it looks bad."

It got cold down in Denver, and fast. I was surprised, and so was Alice. We decided not to go to the library but rather spend the afternoon reading in my living room. She was reading an early book by Pearl Buck, and I got out my copy of *The Good Earth* so that we'd be reading the same author at the same time. I thought that was kind of neat.

"You know, those poor Chinese peasants have suffered so. And the women with their bound feet. I'm glad we live in this country," Alice said.

What an odd thing for her to say. It brought to my mind that she had never mentioned Jane's terrible letter. Well, yes, she had in a way. She'd tried to soothe me. Perhaps she would have said more if Len hadn't interrupted us that day. Of course, she couldn't bring it up herself after that. The right moment always passed.

Early Saturday evening, Leah called. "Where is Father? I want to talk to both of you!" She was thrilled about something.

"He isn't here. He's gone for the weekend. I'll have him call you tomorrow evening. What is it that can't wait?"

"Father's gone? How weird. I'm going to get married."

"What? You're going to get married? Are you pregnant?"

"Not *get* married. I mean *be* married. I'm taking this course in Third World Communication. There's this guy in it who's really cute—blond hair, blue eyes, a great smile." She was silent for a moment and then seemed to giggle at someone. "I thought he was so cute I bought some cookies in the vending machine and offered him one. He loved that. He took me out to lunch, and halfway through he said, 'I'm going to marry you.' He's a lot like Earnest Hemingway; he wants to be a journalist—'Yes, you!'" she said to someone else, and then turned back to me.

"Does he have a name?" I asked, astonished.

"Robin Pierpoint III. Isn't that a fabulous name? He graduated from Yale, and now he's here learning journalism."

"Oh. Has he *asked* you to marry him?"

"Yes, Mo-THER! You don't believe me, do you?"

"This is all so sudden. Why haven't you told me about dating someone? Don't we talk anymore?"

"All you've talked about lately is Jane's, er, 'ethnic-minority boyfriend,' as we say in my communication class."

"Oh, God," I said. I felt myself closing my eyes tight. She's bringing *him* up now.

"Well, here he is, here's Robin," she said brightly, pushing him on me, right then and there.

A young, rather high male voice got on the telephone. "Hello, Mrs. Hope. Leah has told me a great deal about you. All great things, of course," he said smoothly. "How are you today?"

"I'm fine." I was oh so careful.

"Leah's coming to my parents' home for Christmas. We're all really looking forward to it."

"Oh—and where are you from?"

"Palos Verdes. That's a community of Los Angeles. I'm sure you and Mr. Hope will go there soon to meet my family. We're all going to enjoy each other so much in the years to come."

Leah took the phone back. "Actually, I'm not in my attic place. I'm over at Robin's house in Palo Alto. This is his phone. I'm making dinner for him tonight. I'm having chicken cordon bleu, Italian wine, and peach flambé. Then we'll sip Cointreau."

"What vegetable are you having?"

"Oh, I hadn't thought about that."

"Well, I don't know what to say, Leah, I don't know what to say."

"You never do. You could be happy for us." She paused. "We're going to have six kids. I've got to think about cooking now. Goodbye."

Alice couldn't have helped hearing the gist of it.

"Alice, I don't know whether to laugh or cry," I admitted.

"Well ..." She thought for a moment. 'You and I and our daughters ... oh, let's have some sherry, Anne, and then we can make dinner together. I'll go get things for a salad from my kitchen."

We could fix vegetables, I thought, laughing to myself at Leah's silly menu.

When Alice came back a few minutes later, I'd already taken some chicken out of the refrigerator and started cubing it, so that between the two of us, we could come up with chicken salad. Len and Charles had taken with them everything substantial, like the sliced ham and the package of hamburger.

"Gosh, it's cold out there all of a sudden!" said Alice. "And the wind—look at the tree branches sway. I noticed coming back over here that there are thick snow clouds over the mountains."

While Alice was mixing the salad together and stirring in mayonnaise, I called the ranch.

"It's been snowing hard since about two o'clock. You should hear the wind," Len said with the gusto people feel as big weather hits. "We've got a real snowstorm going."

"Oh, Leonard."

"Don't the two of you worry about a thing. Even if the electricity goes out, we've got plenty of your heavy blankets, and the kerosene lamps."

"Oh, I'm so worried. Charles isn't used to this."

"Charles and I are having a good old time. Right now we're having beer. Here, I'll put the man on and you get Alice."

Alice spoke with Charles. She laughed while they talked. "Ten inches already. So thick you can hardly see the truck," she repeated. "Well, you can tell us all about it tomorrow evening, in front of a nice warm fire."

Then Alice and I looked at each other and laughed. I dished up the chicken salad. She said, "I'll bet they secretly want the electricity to go out. They sound like kids spending the night in a tent somewhere—adventure!"

After our dinner in the dinette, Alice and I each put on one of my housecoats and took our bottle of sherry out to the living room sofa, to watch the weather through the picture window. Snow was coming down in a slant. It was sleek silver in front of the alley lights. Driven by the wind, the snow was accumulating in the joints of the oak tree's empty branches and at their juncture with the youthful trunk. Except for the wind, the world was silent. Life was crisp and exciting, yet cozy.

"I feel safe as a bug in a rug," I announced, filling my glass. The thought made me giggle for some reason.

"What was Robin like? What did he sound like?" Alice asked.

"He sounded polite. Like he knew what to say. Like that was easy. He must have picked that up at Yale."

"But *what* did he sound like?"

"He didn't sound like anything. He just sounded like politeness. Nothing personal. I guess he was, well, trite."

"Oh?"

"A trite young man." I laughed and laughed.

"That doesn't sound like Leah's kind at all."

"Oh, you're completely right, Alice. You're completely right." I felt tears in my eyes. I wondered if I was allergic to something in the chicken salad, or the sherry.

"Leah is such a free spirit. Like our Susan."

Odd as it might sound, I had never realized Alice and I were the same mother to the same daughter. My eyes became fuller. Then a tear slipped down my cheek. "There is something about Leah. I sometimes worry she's going to be the tragedy of my life."

"What on earth do you mean, Anne?" Alice poured a bit more into my glass as she leaned toward me. The bottle of sherry had been sitting in front of her on the coffee table. Now it was sitting in front of me.

I looked at the ceiling and placed the tip of my tongue on my upper lip. I took a breath. "She almost had a nervous breakdown."

"What ..."

"Three years ago. I had to fly to Stanford and put a stop to it."

"How on earth did you do that?"

"I sat her down and read to her from *The Prophet*. She was pretty far gone. I don't know what would have happened if that hadn't worked. I just don't know."

Alice took my two hands in hers.

"Anne, what a beautiful engagement ring you have."

Imagine that.

I looked in her eyes. "Thank you, Alice. I've never really been sure about it. Thank you." I paused, then added, "I wonder what rings Jane and Leah will be getting."

There, I had mentioned it.

Then I was tired. Alice must have been tired, too, because she said, "Let's call Charles and Len before I go back."

We walked to the kitchen, to the phone. I dialed.

The ranch phone was dead.

We looked at each other, each of us putting her hand over her mouth. Suddenly I realized I was cold. Alice held her shoulders.

"Of course, they'll be all right," I said. "They're both ranchers. Do you want to sleep here?"

"No," Alice said. "Maybe the phone will go on again and Charles will try to call me. I know that sounds silly. Anyway, one of my children might call too. And I never know when Susan's going to call in the middle of the night. I just have to be there for her. And of course, there are the two dogs."

I went right to sleep.

Sunday morning, I lay in bed and felt a sharp, nasty headache. That had never happened to me before. I suddenly realized it was the sherry. Then I hoped I hadn't said something wrong in front of Alice.

It kept snowing all morning. Around noon, the weather report on the radio said the state plows had reopened Highway 285, the highway that went within four miles of the ranch. That was good news; now it was just a matter of time until the county road was cleared and Len could plow with his tractor's blade out to it, to make a path for the baby-blue truck.

I imagined the vastness of the snow up there, the whitened forests, the meadows with their gentle dips and rises smoothed out into otherworldly sameness. The nearness of the covered sky, everything startlingly cold, especially the cold wind on the two men's unprotected faces as they set about plowing their way out. I pictured them gaining a foot, five feet, fifty feet on the narrow lane up the hill to the county road. It would be a full day of hard work. In the middle of the afternoon, the wind would die down and the sky's clabbery thickness would begin to shimmer a bit, then a lot, and the sun looking cold like a moon would appear and within minutes begin to shine golden, and as Len and Charles looked around, the color of the sky would be a dazzling blue and the vast snow everywhere would glisten. Fairyland.

Vigorous but exhausted, Len looked like a sort of raccoon when I saw him come in the side door at about six o'clock. They'd found two bandanas in the coat closet at the cabin to protect the lower half of their faces from the wind and the cold. They'd pulled the hoods of their winter coats down to their eyebrows. On either side of Len's eyes, the skin was bright red.

I'd seen that much happiness on him only once before—the morning when he'd gotten that management job. But today, tired as he was, he walked both higher and sturdier than ever before. He'd become the man he'd been meant to be. Of course, he didn't know that, but I did. Too bad Jane wasn't there to see him swagger. So good Leah wasn't there, confusing the moment somehow.

What if he'd always been so happy? I mean here and there, now and then; nobody's happy all the time. But here he was now—three-dimensional, in color, his voice low and solid.

How would my life have been with such a husband?

How indeed?

"We had a hell of a good time. That Charles Thatcher is a real talker. He told me about the whole world. They've been everywhere. Not all the way around the world like that old babe Virginia, but at least Charles has the brains to know what he was looking at. They even saw Queen Elizabeth, imagine that! And that Charles is a good worker. I showed him how to drive the tractor, and he was a whiz at it. I couldn't have plowed out without him."

"Yes, you could have," I said firmly.

That made him stop. He grinned to himself.

"How much wood did you get?"

Len put his head back and laughed. His raccoon skin crinkled. "None. How were we supposed to clean all the snow off the wood and put it in the pickup in the middle of a blizzard?"

We both laughed.

"Alice will find that funny too," I said.

"By the way, your daughter's engaged," I added.

"I'm not surprised. And no, I didn't talk to Charles about it. It's none of his damn business."

"No, I mean your other daughter. Leah."

He stood there in his stocking feet and smelly clothes and thought for a moment. "Now what the hell is going on?"

"His name is Robin Pierpoint III, and he's from Yale. He has blond hair and blue eyes."

I said that kind of like a triumphant parent, but also with a little giggle at the absurdity of it all.

"Leah?"

"Yes, Leah."

Len immediately got to the point, as he saw it. "Is his family rich?"

"Len, I don't know. I suppose so."

He shook his head in disbelief. "Well, I'll be damned." He walked out of the kitchen, presumably to take a hot shower.

After he left, I giggled at my husband as well.

That night I could almost feel Len still tingling from his wonderful weekend as he settled into his bed beside mine. That half of the room was at peace.

Oddly, I felt too warm to sleep. I pulled back my covers and lay underneath just my sheet. I listened for sounds. I looked out the window, through a corner beside the drapes, at the accumulated snow, vaguely opalescent from the street lights. *It would be a good time to have a cat*, I reflected.

How could anyone marry Leah? What would that take away from her? She deserved not to be tamed. I realized I loved her five-thousand language flashcards, her burgundy handbag, the idea of her making peach flambé.

In April, she left him.

"Oh, yeah, it's over," she said by way of explanation.

And that was the end of that.

17

I'd just put on my blue nightgown and was on my way to the bathroom to brush my teeth. I picked up the phone by my bed.

"Hi.... It's me ..." A voice like a child all alone.

I was a little irritated. Whatever it was, Leah knew I'd be heading for bed right then.

Len and I'd been almost-quarreling over dinner then, picking it up and letting it go all evening, as we sat in the living room. Jane wanted to come home for the summer, after she got back from the Peace Corps, to take some remedial courses at CU so she could follow her boyfriend off to graduate school. Her staying with us for the summer was fine with me, but I didn't want her boyfriend coming. Len saw nothing really wrong with the boyfriend, especially since he was trying to better himself by going to graduate school.

"But what will the neighbors think?" I asked Len.

"If the two of them want each other that badly, it will happen no matter you objecting."

"Don't you care?" I said loudly, my foot jerking.

Every time we exchanged words about it, it came to that: he just didn't seem to care. Or maybe he didn't see anything wrong. To be frank, that angered me more. At about nine o'clock, he'd ended it by telling me to relax. I'd closed my eyes and sat in silence, head bowed. He'd gone out to the patio to fume alone. We both knew it wasn't finished. And now this.

"What is it, Leah? Why are you calling this late?" I asked.

"I want Father on the phone too."

"He's outside in the back. I'm not dressed ..."

"Please," she pleaded. Her voice was hollow.

I cocked my head at her strangeness and went out to open the back door just a crack, so the neighbors across the alley wouldn't see my nightgown, and whispered loudly so Len could hear me over the train in the distance. "Len, Leah's on the phone. She wants to talk to you. I don't know why, at this hour."

"Leah?" he asked. He put his cigar on the arm of the wicker chair. He came in and picked up the extension in the kitchen. "Now what is going on with you, at this hour?"

"I'm in the hospital. I tried to kill myself." Hesitant, small.

Kill herself? *Kill herself?* I saw Leah covered in blood. Who had found her? I saw her unconscious, in an ambulance. Why hadn't doctors called me right away? What was going on? My blood pressure soared; my chest felt like it had no room left to breathe in. I was afraid I was going to have a heart attack.

Len said quietly, "Do you want your mother to come?"

"I don't know," Leah said flatly. "She can come."

"I don't know." Like she was talking beyond us.

"Do you want your mother to come tomorrow?" Len asked again.

"I don't know. They told me here that I had to call you." Her voice threatened a scream.

My daughter had never talked that way in her life. What was this about anyway?

Leah's confused. Something is awful.

"We're coming tomorrow," I said, recovering my voice.

"I'm sorry," she said.

"Well, this is very bad news," Len said, coming into the bedroom. His voice was still quiet.

"We're going to have to go there," I said.

"You can go tomorrow morning."

I looked at him hard. "Both of us."

I watched that sink in.

"Well, let's not stand here talking about it," he said, looking at the floor. "I'll call the office. The evening crew's there. I can be gone tomorrow, maybe the next day."

Maybe all she needs is a talking to, he seemed to be saying.

"I'll have to come back, but maybe you'll want to stay a while," he added. "Call the Thatchers. It's not too late to call. Tell them we can't have dinner tomorrow evening."

"What shall I tell them?"

"I don't know!"

"I'll tell them … that something's come up. You tell them at the office that something's come up. Let's keep our stories straight." Us bewildered, facing things without known solutions. "I don't know what we're supposed to do."

"And I don't have any money," Len said. I could feel anger toward Leah in his confusion. "We'd be gone before the bank opens."

"It's all right. It'll be all right." Money didn't matter to me just then.

"Even if you went alone, how would you pay for the bus from the airport to Palo Alto? And a taxi from Palo Alto to the hospital?"

"You're coming with me. Period. This is your daughter too."

He had a look on his face like he'd just realized that. "Well, at least they'll feed us breakfast on the plane," he said.

We floundered among details.

"What if she's not all right?" I asked. I didn't have the slightest idea what that would mean, only that it would be the whole world slamming us in the face.

"She'll be all right."

"Len, your daughter said she tried to kill herself."

"Well, that's what she said."

We left the house at 3:00 a.m., thick with tiredness, cross with each other over every little thing. I wore my gray skirt and an ordinary white blouse, Len in one of his two everyday suits. Two suitcases, not one, in case Len came back before me. He had thirty-five dollars. I had five. We were going to the Stanford Hospital.

On the plane, we sat alone in first class with our employee passes. The seats were so wide, the stewardess extra-attentive. I realized I'd forgotten earrings.

The world was still black outside the window. Len sat beside it, looking out. There was no one but us in the cabin, no sound but the engines throbbing evenly, so I ventured to say something. "Do you suppose we did anything wrong? I can't think of anything we did wrong."

"We did nothing wrong."

"I don't think we did either. Except for that time you beat her up so badly. Do you suppose that caused it?"

He breathed sharply and closed his eyes. "But she was being so obstinate!"

See, he still remembered it as much as I did. So long ago, everything out of control, the three of us stunned in the aftermath.

All the years I'd been married to Len, I'd often watched his hands. When he was working, turning a nut on a bolt with a wrench, cutting wire with pliers—those were his hands in thick workman's gloves. I'd seen his gloveless hands too, wielding a ballpoint pen with his slanting, doubled-back left hand. I'd also seen him tie his shoelaces, and hold the evening paper over his lap. Now I was remembering his hand picking up Leah by the shoulder that time when she was so small, throwing her into the living room couch, starting the beating.

Then there was me. From time to time he'd silently touch me with invisible hands in the dark. Or sometimes during the day, he'd jokingly pat me on top of the head with his hand, and then laugh at my anger. But now his hands were just there on his thighs. He was clenching them tightly, and the knuckles stuck out white, and the blue veins stood up. His hands trembled a little.

The San Francisco airport was just getting its start on the day, coffee shops opening, the newspapers in big bundles by the stands, the shoe shiners setting up.

We spent most of the money we had between us on the bus ride to Palo Alto from the airport. The express bus headed down the Peninsula, past the towns on the right and left of the freeway: Burlington, Redwood City, Menlo Park.

Len got us a taxi at the little Palo Alto terminal. "We want to go to the Stanford Hospital."

The palm trees, the red roofs and yellow buildings in morning light—I'd been in this world before, now and then across the years. But this time was different.

I'd never seen the hospital before. Its appearance was jolting: a huge, white, modern building at the far end of campus. It was far too imposing for a young girl to be in, in some bed somewhere. At the front desk, the young man in white said they had no patient by her name.

We stared in disbelief. "She's our daughter. She goes to school here!"

The young man thought for a moment, made a phone call, and then said our daughter was in the student infirmary, across campus.

"I'm sorry, but we've come all the way from Denver, and we didn't have time to get money before we came, and now we can't afford the taxi ride over there," I blurted.

The young man handed me five dollars.

I did not feel like a beggar.

We passed a gift shop on the way out. It had just opened. I walked in and chose a vase of pink tea-rose buds.

"My daughter is very ill. We have no cash. Would you take two dollars out of this?" I asked the young woman. I handed her the five-dollar bill.

MY MOTHER'S AUTOBIOGRAPHY

We saw Leah just after she'd had breakfast. She was wearing blue jeans and her gray "J.S. Bach" t-shirt. She lay in a bed, the back raised. She had a bandage on one wrist, a Band-Aid on the other.

She looked at us from different eyes. She stared at the roses and cringed. "I don't deserve these," she said, her thin voice cracking.

I bent over her. "May I hug you, Leah?"

"No. You hate me."

Len stood there in the middle of the room, by her feet. His hands were in his pockets, and he looked at the floor. "I don't know what to say," he said softly.

Then I noticed Leah was shaking all over, shaking hard. "Are you cold?"

"I don't know."

"How was breakfast?" I asked her, to keep talk going.

"I don't know."

The white-clad nurse came and, weirdly, took her temperature and felt her pulse. She left.

"What can I do for you, Leah?" I begged.

"I don't know." Then she said, "They're trying to slice my eyeballs with razor blades."

What? A mind not her own, in this white room like a foreign land. Terrified, I glanced at Len. He didn't seem to have heard it.

The nurse came back and stopped in front of my husband. "The doctors are ready to see all of you as a family in the conference room."

The three of us went in a row, led by the nurse. It was about nine o'clock.

In the conference room, big chairs were arranged in a loose circle. There was no table. Everyone shook hands. Mrs. Hunter introduced herself as Leah's social worker. She was a little plump, with thick black hair pulled away from her face in a large bun, and she wore thick-rimmed black glasses. Dr. Pauley, the psychiatrist, was pink and fat and wore a brown suit. They both looked fresh, just starting their days.

Len's suit pants were wrinkled now, and I had a run in one of my stockings.

We sat down. Leah wouldn't sit between us. She shook.

Dr. Pauley's first words were to me. "Did you want Leah, Mrs. Hope?"

I jerked back in my chair, horrified. "W-well, yes," I stammered. "We already had one daughter, and we didn't want her to be alone …"

I was stunned at that accusation. Of course I had wanted my daughter. I had carried her, brought her forth in pain. Here he was, like I had no feelings at all, asking me the very question a mother could never bear to hear.

"When you were growing up, did you feel like they wanted you, Leah?" Mrs. Hunter asked.

"She hit me. She hit me all the time. All the time!" Leah said in one breath. "She knocked me down and grabbed my neck and hit my head against the floor!"

"That's not true, that's not true at all," I gasped.

All eyes on me. I got up and put my coat over Leah's shoulders. She still shook.

"Does anything else make you unhappy, Leah?" Dr. Pauley continued.

"Everything."

"Like what?"

"There's no justice in the world. We're in that horrible war in Vietnam. They've just killed Bobby Kennedy. And look at the Negroes, the riots, the injustice. Look at the way they're treated in America. Look what they did to Martin Luther King!"

Len spoke gently, as though to a small child. "The Negroes are a happy people.... They have their music..."

Leah put her hands to her ears.

Dr. Pauley asked her what she wanted everyone to do for her.

"I don't know. Stop the razor blades."

"What does that mean?" I said.

"It means she's very angry," Dr. Pauley said. He turned back to Leah. "Do you want to go home with your parents?"

"No—not with her." Her eyes intense, darting. Like they were trying to escape something.

"What's wrong with my daughter? Isn't there some medicine for this?" I asked.

"No. Problems like Leah's are almost inevitably caused by family dynamics."

Len and I looked at each other. What were "family dynamics"?

"We're hoping, of course, that you and your husband will be getting psychotherapy as well. Especially you, Mrs. Hope," Dr. Pauley concluded.

"There must be some medicine." I was near tears.

"Mrs. Hope, there is no medicine."

"There *is* a medicine. I know there is some medicine, somewhere."

Dr. Pauley raised his eyebrows, and asked, "What medical school did you go to, Mrs. Hope?"

I was helpless against his slick words. I closed my eyes so I wouldn't cry.

All five of us sat silent, Leah shaking, until Len said, "Dr. Pauley, I have no money with me because this was so sudden. Could I possibly write you a check? Would fifty dollars be possible?"

Dr. Pauley got his wallet out of his jacket and checked his money. "That would be fine," he said.

Len had no choice about doing that. He trembled as he wrote. Then, the two men shook hands over the transaction.

"Is she going to be all right?" I asked no one in particular. My voice was so small I didn't think anyone heard it.

"Yes, she's going to be all right," Mrs. Hunter replied in a kind voice.

Len walked with me differently as we left the infirmary. He had been cited for nothing, really. I was stinging from blame by my daughter, her social worker, her psychiatrist, and now, as he walked ahead of me, seemingly by my husband.

What had happened to my daughter? What were they doing to me? I wanted to put my hands over my ears, as Leah had in the conference room.

We took a cab down El Camino Real and stopped at the first motel Len saw. He looked it over and said it would do, so he went in and took a room. It had Spanish-style furniture, including an obscenely big bed with a burgundy bedspread. The air conditioning chilled me until I almost started shaking like Leah.

There was a modern coffee shop next door. With some of the money from Dr. Pauley, we had sandwiches and coffee.

I was too tired to be hungry, so Len ate the second half of my sandwich. He chewed at it angrily.

A woman at the front desk in the motel arranged for Len to rent a car.

That afternoon, having changed our shirts but still in our rumpled suit and skirt, we went in the new-smelling, too-large car to see Leah again. She was oh so frail. I asked her how much she weighed.

"About a hundred pounds," Leah said, and she was a tall girl. We took her to Blum's, an ice cream parlor over in the Palo Alto shopping center. There was nothing else we could think to do for her. She ordered a double butterscotch ice-cream sundae.

I was sure all the ladies in their fine suits, store bags at their feet, were watching us as we stared silently at Leah eating voraciously.

For half an hour, she shook less.

Back at the infirmary, Leah kicked off her shoes and got under the covers, pulling them up around her face.

Len said, "Well, I think if we just get you out of here and find you a job, you'll settle in and your life will be much calmer."

Leah began crying. She couldn't stop. She cried until she gasped for air between spasms of crying. Len and I stood on each side of her, embracing her, and she couldn't stop.

The nurse came, then Mrs. Hunter. Mrs. Hunter urged her to breathe deeply, hold a breath, breathe deeply again.

Leah's t-shirt clung to her, wet with her tears when she came to a stop.

Mrs. Hunter had the nurse pull up chairs for all of us. "Leah, can you promise me you won't try again to kill yourself?"

"No."

"No you can't?"

"No."

"Do you mean, no you won't?"

Leah didn't move in any way except to breathe. Her face was tight with woe. But her eyes were terrified.

"We can't just let you go. We have a legal responsibility. There's a sanitarium nearby, in Belmont. We've sent other people to it, with good results. What do you think? Would you like to go there?"

Leah's face visibly relaxed.

I was stunned by that. It made no sense at all.

I don't exactly remember when Len and Mrs. Hunter left the room together. Something about making arrangements. I was alone with Leah.

"You want to go there, don't you?" I asked her softly.

"Yes."

"That's what she wants!" I yelled at Len, back in the motel room. "She wants to go to a mental hospital!"

Len sat on the edge of the huge bed and cried. He crossed his arms while he cried, so I wasn't able to see his hands. He cried.

"And you're to blame for all of this!" he shouted at me through his tears.

"I ... am not to blame ... for ... anything."

"That doctor and that woman as much as said you are to blame for the whole thing."

"So now I'm the fall guy, am I?"

"You've never taken the blame for anything in your life."

"Well, neither have you, and there's been a lot of things you've done wrong, mister!"

He jumped to his feet, put his furious face up to mine, and flung his arm out, hand wide open. Just as suddenly, he dropped it. Then he picked up the heavy, garish lamp and knocked it down into its nightstand. The bulb broke and scattered glass.

In a worn-out voice, weirdly like Leah's current one, he said, "This isn't solving anything. I'm going on a drive."

When he left, I bent down and picked pieces of delicate glass off the beige carpet. Bitterly, I wrapped them in a tissue, so no one cleaning the room would get cut.

18

So much had begun happening to our family. At first it was just circus oddities and grotesqueries, but then brave tigers leapt through fiery hoops, catching themselves on fire and racing silent and panicked around and around the tent, enflaming it, trapping us all inside.

Len went home the very next day, Thursday, to return to his job. He would be unable to tell anyone at work—or even the Thatchers—where he'd been. He had two realities, two stories to keep straight. Who did he have to help him?

Jane would be arriving in New York that evening. Was Len resentful that it would fall to him to tell her the truth?

He'd left everything here in Palo Alto on my shoulders. Leah's books, clothing, bank account, her clutter. She even, somehow, owned an antique chest of drawers. How was I to get hold of boxes, mail things? What about that chest of drawers?

And a cat! I was alone, forced to do things that I should have been able to ask Len to do, husbandly things.

I went to see Leah later that morning. I wore the other outfit I'd packed, my brown-and-white pantsuit. It was an everyday thing, just a pantsuit, but it was all I had, and anyway Mrs. Hunter couldn't look down her nose at me anymore than she already did.

Leah turned away when she saw me come in the room. I took her wrists, to kiss her two wounds. She pulled back.

"Let me kiss you, Leah."

She closed her eyes, raised her chin, and inhaled sharply.

I didn't know how to kiss her. After all, she was an adult. And we'd never been a kissing family. I fumbled, and my kiss fell on her lips. We were both embarrassed.

"You never touched me, growing up. Except when you hit me," Leah said.

I bit my lip hard and turned my head to the wall.

The nurse took us to Mrs. Hunter's office at 10 a.m. She'd made the phone calls, arranged our arrival at the sanitarium for Friday.

"I can't tell whether you can't or you won't promise not to hurt yourself again. That leaves me no choice but to recommend this," Mrs. Hunter said to my daughter.

Shaking, Leah looked through her.

Thursday evening, late, I was lying on top of that burgundy bedspread in the motel, tired and angry at that horrible doctor and that woman, so terrified for Leah that I felt panicky.

Jane called me from *her* hotel room in New York. Len had given her the phone number of mine. She was exhausted from her trip from North Africa; she'd had a layover of six hours in London, then accommodations confusion in the hotel at the JFK airport. She could not, I figured, have been more tired. I pictured her lying on her big hotel bed, holding the phone to her face. She had her genuine, earnest, naïve voice—which hadn't changed a bit—when she said, "Mother, it's me …"

I shouted at her. "Leah's going to a mental hospital tomorrow!"

Jane drew her breath in slowly, then was completely silent.

In the awkwardness that followed, I felt Jane backing up, backing up, her hand over her mouth, backing up from me. I imagined her eyes big and glaring, filled with scorn, like her scorn at the Arab cart-owners who'd driven their horses to exhaustion and starvation, still whipping them, yelling at them.

She said that was too bad about Leah, and then whispered she was too tired to talk. She said goodbye and hung up.

What was I supposed to have said?

I saw Mrs. Hunter in my mind's eye, asking me if I had wanted my child. I stuck my chin up, closed my eyes, and cringed at myself.

Friday afternoon, I drove Leah, still in her blue jeans and "J.S. Bach" t-shirt, to the hospital. The car Len had rented didn't have a stick shift. I could barely maneuver it. It crossed my mind that I didn't know what you do with a rental car when you're done with it. I got lost, because all the stupid little towns looked the same. I couldn't tell if I was going up El Camino Real to San Francisco, or down it to San Jose. How did you ask for directions here? After a while, I wondered in all seriousness if I would run out of gas and what would happen then. I had

135

to get hold of myself, so I pulled off to the side in a no-parking zone. Leah had no reaction. Someone stopped who was walking by, a young man. There was a weird smell in the air around him.

"Oh, that's pot. Pot—marijuana," he laughed. Then he laughed some more at my shocked face. "Yes, you're going in the right direction, lady."

The place we were going to was in the little town of Belmont, north of Palo Alto, up a winding road to an enormous white Victorian mansion that reminded me for an odd moment of a big, fancy Mississippi showboat. I turned in, passed through a gate, and drove up a pebbled drive. A white-clad nurse met our car and escorted us to an office where an older, professional woman introduced herself to me. Her gentle eyes struck me as kind and utterly out of place. She explained procedures and had me sign some papers. I was terrified. I couldn't understand the papers, didn't want to sign my daughter away. Leah was about to go down a long dark tunnel, and the doctors inside might decide she had to stay there for years, or for the rest of her life.

My daughter sat beside me, shaking and silent and aware of everything, even though her eyes were looking somewhere else. The professional saw how thin she was and asked her if she'd like to have a milkshake. When Leah nodded, a male nurse took her away. "We'll make sure she gets two milkshakes a day," the woman said reassuringly.

The words "two milkshakes a day" and Leah's distant silence remained in the air as I stood up, shaking the woman's hand.

Leah hadn't even said goodbye; she'd just gone off into her new world. If she was even still Leah. If she was still my daughter.

I left the white bric-a-brac mansion behind me and drove back into Belmont. I stopped the car at the first phone booth I saw. The folding glass and metal door wouldn't close all the way. Inside, on the floor, was an empty red can. The compartment smelled of cigarettes; I got out a tissue to hold the receiver with. I called Len at his office.

When I heard his bland "Hello …" I yelled, "I just put Leah in that hospital. Maybe they won't even let her out again, ever! Maybe they'll give her electroshock treatments and destroy her mind. Maybe they'll even give her a lobotomy. This is too much. I'm going to have a heart attack right now!"

I let the receiver fall to the floor of the little booth and stood there sobbing. Everyone driving by or walking down the sidewalk would surely have heard me shouting, seen me through the glass panels, bent over with my face in my hands. No one stopped.

I felt like I was being electrocuted. I drove down the hill and turned left onto El Camino Real. I'd run out of tissues and my eyes and nose were dripping liquid all over my face. I wiped it off my cheeks and mouth with my bare hand. Cars were going too fast. I gripped the steering wheel and sniffed and hacked and knew none of this would ever end. A green sign for San Mateo passed on my right, then everything looked the same for miles, and I had to go to the bathroom. The feeling, of course, was going to get worse and worse. I'd have to go off on an unknown side road to find a gas station where I could relieve myself. Get lost trying to get back on El Camino. Not remember which way to go. But there was no choice in the matter.

A green sign for Burlingame.

Right after it, a big sign read, "San Francisco International Airport, right three miles."

I was going in the wrong direction.

I turned into the Burlingame exit, drove past a gas station, turned back to it and walked hard into its public bathroom. Again, grime everywhere. I pushed on the toilet handle with one finger, and then the water spigot, wiping my wet hands on my brown trousers. On my way back to the car I was asked by a kindly young woman, "Are you all right, lady?"

I realized my hands were fists and my mouth was open.

I got in the car without acknowledging her and drove back to El Camino. A San Mateo sign—I sighed in relief. Then a Belmont sign. I didn't look over. Somewhere up there was a huge white showboat on a hill.

Minutes later, I spotted tan Hoover Tower over in the distance, to the right. It was so ugly, like a big vertical cigar.

I was still clutching the steering wheel hard. Then I was coming upon that university, that Stanford I'd disliked for years now, with all its red tile roofs on fake Spanish buildings.

Suddenly I thought of Alice Thatcher and her daughter, Susan. We could shed tears together, Alice and I.

I arrived at this trip's motel. In my three days here its name hadn't even registered with me. I saw now it was the California Dream Motel: "Welcome to our hospitality and convenience."

I pulled into the parking lot, right by the lobby door. I shook my hands to loosen them after all that gripping, put my head back, and closed my eyes. Then I heard voices nearby, so I sat up straight. The concierge, in an olive-green uniform and white tie, came to the lobby door with two policemen in black, with holsters. The concierge pointed at me.

"Are you Mrs. Hope?" one policeman bent down and asked.

"Yes, I am …"

"Your husband is looking for you. It seems he thought you'd collapsed, but he didn't know where. 'Could have been anywhere,' he said. We've been told he was worried."

I closed my eyes and sucked in my lips, mortified at myself. "I'm very, very sorry. There was a misunderstanding …"

"Why don't you go call your husband right away," the policeman said.

"Yes, yes, I'm so sorry."

When they had left, the concierge came over. "An older-sounding woman from Belmont has been calling, too. I have her number inside. And Mr. Hope wants you to call him at home as soon as possible."

When I closed the door of my room behind me, I realized I was shaking, like Leah and Len had. And once again, the maid had turned the air-conditioning so high that the room was freezing. I took my nylons and my panties off and climbed under the covers of the bed.

Were the bedspreads in all the El Camino Real motels burgundy?

I called the woman from Belmont. It was the sanitarium. Len had called there while he was searching for me. I felt like I was disturbing the woman from something, the way she talked. I was so embarrassed. I wondered if it would get back somehow to Mrs. Hunter.

Then I called Len, at home.

"Where have you been? What took you so long?" he asked.

"I got lost coming back."

"Are you all right?" he said slowly, his voice a dead monotone.

"Yes, yes." Silence. I could feel his anger coming over the phone.

"So you said you were going to have a heart attack. Then all I heard was the phone buzzing. Did you just stand there? Didn't you hear me yelling?"

Freezing cold and sticky all over, at the end of my line—no, of his—and I was guilty. This time it was my own husband, not some arrogant doctor.

"I'm sorry," I said softly. I realized that was the first time I'd ever said that to him.

"Just what kind of a position do you think that put me in? Here I was calling all over the place from my office, trying to get help. I finally came home, in case someone would try to call me here." He stopped to catch his breath. "Well, there's going to be hell to pay, let me tell you. Jane just got home. She's dead tired. She's already in bed."

Jane. Suddenly, Jane.

"Well, I'm just going to say goodbye," he said. Then he hung up on me.

I pulled the cover over my head and lay there listening to my heart beating. I almost wished I had died in that phone booth in Belmont. But I didn't really, *really* want to be dead. Dead could be real. Between me and that was a lot of fear. I pushed it away—the death, I mean, and the fear. I was only months away from being fifty-five years old, and I could not yet face that much fear. I would put that off until another point in my life.

Slowly, I became aware of the room I was in. Of its air that was beginning to warm, of the sunlight growing weaker outside, of the sounds in the hall and in the parking lot. Of the fact that I hadn't eaten since breakfast.

It was 7:00 p.m. I put my panties back on and went back down to the lobby. In a corner, by the stand with the free coffee and Cremora and sugar packets, there was a candy machine and a machine with cookies and Danish pastries. I got two Danishes and a cup of hot water and a tea bag, and went back up to my room.

Leah. In the big, white, mansion hospital.

I got my pieces of paper with phone numbers on them and called there. I had to remember to call it a sanitarium, not a hospital.

I wanted my daughter so very badly.

I was told I could not talk to Leah for seventy-two hours. Seventy-two hours of observation. Seventy-two hours of being allowed to adjust to her new surroundings. She was doing fine, the nurse said, and added a good night.

19

Jane was late. But that was all right; it's hard to judge when to get to Arrivals just in time to scoop your passenger into the car. Maybe there'd been a lot of traffic.

I stood on the curb at Arrivals, coat draped over my arm, suitcase full of dirty clothes—I'd been gone two weeks—and Leah's cat in a carrier, which I'd bought for it just that morning at a pet store on El Camino. There was a shop for everything on El Camino Real. The cat was yowling, repetitively.

I saw Jane the same moment she saw me. I saw her toss her head, change lanes, swing right in front of me on the curb. She didn't get out.

I opened the passenger door, slung my suitcase onto the back seat, and positioned the carrier beside it. Once he'd gotten out of the airport and airplane noise, Leah's cat fell thankfully silent.

"Jane ..." I said softly. Her dark-brown hair was still long, and she was still thin, but she no longer had the virgin face she'd left with.

"Jane," I said again, and reached over toward her.

"I've got to get out of all this traffic," she said, raising her voice and turning her face over her other shoulder.

Once Jane was clear and out onto the terminal street again, she tossed her head a second time. She sighed deeply, like she was beginning an ordeal, and her hands gripped the wheel until her knuckles showed white.

"Jane, please pull over."

She swerved back to the curb, stopping just short of the last Arrivals door, and turned toward me.

"Jane, I'm so glad to see you—finally!"

"Yes, *Jane.*' At least you haven't forgotten my name."

"I'm so sorry I wasn't there when you got home."

My daughter finally looked me full in the face. Her lips tight and her eyebrows raised, it was clear she was dismissing me. "So, how is Leah?" she asked flatly, and got back out on the street.

"You'll have to ask your father. She won't speak to me."

We had left Stapleton Airport behind and were headed west on the highway. I could see the Rocky Mountains, tiny down by Colorado Springs, then stretching rugged and tall all the way across the west, then turning into little zigzags again toward the north. They were slate blue in the distance, snowless, since it was late June.

"By the way, Alan's here," Jane said.

In my kitchen, cat carrier in my arms, I came to a jolting halt. Leah's cat, upended, started yowling.

Alan was sitting in my chair, in my dinette. His legs were crossed, and he was smoking a cigarette.

He tossed down what appeared to be a large comic book, sprang to his feet, thrust out his hand, and said, "Hi. I'm Chinese."

I burst into tears.

"See what I mean?" Jane said to him.

I was crying, not because all that I could see was a wave of longish jet-black hair and a fast-moving arm, but because I was behind enemy lines. In my own neighborhood, with its sweeping, leafy trees and big green lawns. In my own suburban house, which I'd insisted on buying for those two damn girls, and which I'd longed for those last days in the commercialism of El Camino Real. My own kitchen, where I'd fed and eaten with all those horrible people.

Leah wouldn't talk to me, Len was angry at me, Jane hadn't touched me, and Alan had just attacked me.

Wiping my nose—which made Jane wince—I looked down at the table and saw that Alan had been reading *Fritz the Cat*. A grown man with a comic book about a cat? They were all mad, all of them. But was Leah *really* mad? The thought made me want to scream.

I took the carrier—Leah's cat protesting—and went to my room and closed the door. I sat down on the edge of the bed and let the cat out. I was shaking with exhaustion. After all, I'd just reversed my trip *to* California, that terrifying trip in the night to the girl who said she'd tried to kill herself. I'd made a complete circle and come back to a world that was no longer mine in any real way.

Leah's cat looked around, sniffed the air, and slinked back into the safety of his carrier. After a while, Jane knocked once and opened the door. She'd brought the cat a bowl of water.

It grew dark. I heard all their voices, the laughter. Len must have decided to sleep on the sofa. Away from me.

That night though, I slept deeply, and for a long time. But the moment I awoke, I felt shoved against the wall by dread. I wanted nothing to do with the upcoming day and its promise of conflicts in every direction.

I didn't have long to wait.

It was Saturday, so Len was home from United for the weekend. From the kitchen, I could hear him in the garage. I made myself coffee and got out some bread.

My husband came inside wearing his striped overalls, wiping his hands on a red mechanic's cloth. He walked up to me, stood there, and slapped his hand on his thigh.

He was as cold as he'd been when he called me in the motel. "So, you've been lying to us all these years."

I stared at him, a piece of toast in my raised hand.

He sat down, and didn't pull the chair up. "I took a morning off work last week and went down to see Dr. Osborne. Your Dr. Osborne. I told him what you did to Jane and me in that phone booth by that sanitarium."

I put down my toast. I wasn't even fully awake yet. Staring at him in disbelief, I took a sip of coffee. The sun covered me with its rays. I saw that Len was sitting in a shadow.

"What do you mean, you saw Dr. Osborne?" I asked. "That's invasion of privacy. You do know that, don't you?"

"I told him you've been heart-condition-here, heart-attack-there, delicate here, heart-condition-there, all the years I've known you. I asked him just what kind of a 'heart condition' you have."

"And what did he call it, my heart condition?"

"Dr. Osborne said ..." Len bent toward me, "You have absolutely nothing wrong with your heart. Nothing. All these years, you've been making this up."

I was stunned. "Have you told this to Jane?"

"Of course I've told Jane. And I'm going to tell Leah when the time comes."

Dr. Osborne. I realized I was sitting there with my mouth open, staring blankly at Len.

Bitterness feels like bile in your throat. Like looking everyone in the eye and their consequent laughing at you, every one of them, for all you've done for them and given them through the years.

"You'll pay for this. Mark my words," I said.

He stood up. "It's coin collection day, so I'll be gone. Jane and Alan have already gone up to the ranch. They'll be home in time for dinner. You'll be alone all day. You'll want to go to the store. There's nothing in the refrigerator."

He left.

Leah's cat came to my ankles, wreathed them. I picked him up, sat back down in the dinette, and petted him. With everything else going on, I hadn't really examined him before. He was brown-and-cream colored, kind of fat, and he meowed weirdly, like Siamese do. That Pierpoint III boyfriend had given him to Leah when she lived by herself in the rented attic with all the flashcards. Giving your college girlfriend a Siamese cat—what a cute, irresponsible thing to do.

What an irresponsible thing Dr. Osborne had done to me. Hadn't he known how much I counted on him? More than counted on him. I almost ...

The cat yowled and nuzzled my chin.

I was grateful, for a moment. For a cat.

But what would I do without Dr. Osborne? The one man I trusted in the world, trusted with my whole heart. Oh! I meant, "with my very self."

I would write him, tell him. Ask him why he had betrayed me.

I pushed Leah's cat off my lap and went to get a piece of notebook paper from Jane's room. Lined paper with binder holes was the best I could do; I didn't want to use stationary that said "Mile-High Washing Machine Rental" at the top.

Dr. Osborne, I wrote, letter after carefully constructed letter. I could think only of his kind, sure hands, holding his stethoscope to listen to my heart, making notes in my chart. The wisdom and encouragement with which he had guided me through my menopause and that brush with death by bleeding. Damn him. *Dr. Osborne, you have wronged me. Do not consider me your patient any longer. Sincerely, Mrs. Leonard L. Hope.*

I took a longed-for shower.

Then I walked around my house, reacquainting myself with it. Dearest's purple-and-black afghan still on the living room sofa. Leah's bedroom, sun-lit by big windows catty-corner to each other, now occupied by Alan, who was apparently—judging by his clothes tossed here and there and his suitcase open flat exactly in the middle of the room—a slob. I went back to the living room, the picture window showing our backyard, now covered with grass and boasting our beautiful little oak tree.

I went out to the yard. Then, just like the first time I saw her years before, Alice Thatcher was taking out her trash. She saw me, put down the brown bag, came over to the fence, and touched me on the arm. Long and softly. She looked carefully at my face. "Come have coffee with me, Anne."

"Oh, I would love that."

I went over to her backyard, and we walked into her house. She brought out one of her blue English plates and put two Danishes on it, followed by "CU Buffalos" mugs and a carafe of the morning coffee. She remembered I took sugar and cream both. We settled into the dinette. The two yellow dogs came to lie by our feet.

"How *is* Leah?" asked Alice.

I didn't know she knew. But now, clearly, she did. "Did Len tell Charles?"

Len—confiding in another person, someone outside the family—must have been beside himself those days in Denver. That was so unlike him. I felt a bit of sympathy for his near-solitary plight.

"Yes. About her being in a sanitarium in California. That's really all I know. How is she?" Sitting there, bending toward me, sun on her tousled hair, Alice in a way made up for Mrs. Hunter.

I touched Alice's arm, closed my eyes. "I don't know. I don't honestly know anything, except they told Len that Leah is very sick. And she refuses to speak to me."

When I opened my eyes, I saw Alice had closed her eyes too. Then she looked up. "I can't think of anything to say, Anne."

"I am so lost."

"I know you are."

"There is nothing I can do that is right. I wish someone would just tell me how I'm supposed to behave," I said under my breath. I realized I was being bitter.

Had anyone ever told Alice she was a bad mother? I couldn't ask a question like that, of course not.

"Is there some place you'd like to be just now?" she asked.

Something *I'd* want? It had surely been years since anyone had asked that.

I was grateful for the moment. A blue plate. Something sweet on it. The clink of her spoon against her mug, making almost a musical note. My heart swelled. "I'd like to be in my woods, behind my cabin, walking in my forest."

"Then let's go there."

"I can't …"

"Let's go there. We'll change into jeans and leave notes in our kitchens for Charles and Len. We'll call them when we get to your cabin. You can even call the sanitarium from the cabin. I'll take us some sandwiches."

Alice had never been to the ranch. Only Charles had, with Len on that blizzardy weekend. When we got there, Jane's car was in the driveway, but she and Alan were nowhere to be seen. Good. Perhaps they were out hiking on the county road, or had gone to the neighbors' cliffs to see the Cathedral Spires.

"Jane's brought Alan up to see her beloved ranch," I told Alice. "She loves this ranch as much as she did when she was a little girl. She'll always keep coming here. She hates the fact that it was put in my name, which makes me its owner outright. She sees it as her place, hers and her father's. And I suppose, in a way, she's right."

"Well, they won't bother us," Alice said. Then I remembered the time, back in spring, when I'd had Alice read Jane's letter from North Africa about the Chinese boyfriend. No,

Alice had never really commented on that. Except to mention love.

They had opened up the cabin and the window over the sink; the air inside was already smelling fresh. Jane's purse and a picnic lunch were on the big round table in the kitchen. We put our purses down too, staking out a bit of the table. Kind of funny, really.

We sipped cold mountain water from the faucet. "Look out my window here, over the sink," I said. "You can see the black squirrels in the ponderosas. When the girls were young and we stayed up here during summers, I watched out there while I did my dishes, day after day. I came to call them my woods."

"I'd love to go in them with you," Alice said.

So we walked into them, in private silences, the forest debris crackling beneath our feet. Our shoulders loosened, we took to moving in a zigzag, catching one thing after another in our sight.

I stopped at a sawed-off tree, maybe five inches of trunk sticking up from the ground, no longer blond and sappy inside but washed-out gray, so dead even the rings couldn't be counted after ten years' exposure to winters. Old, gnarled branches from the cutting lay around.

"This is where Len cut out the beetle trees one summer. You'll see the flat stumps all through here. Just don't trip on one. And down here," I pointed as we headed east, "are the ruins of Jane and Leah's animal village."

"Oh, look …" Alice said. She walked over and bent down to see the remains of stables and pens made of wooden crates, and plaster-of-paris dogs and cats and horses now so weather-eroded that their features were nearly gone. "Your daughters must have been just little girls then."

"They were. Just little girls. The animal village was a secret between them, but of course I'd gone alone once, at first, to see what they were doing hours on end out here."

We'd reached the middle of the woods. It was darker, cooler there. We realized we'd forgotten sweaters.

"So that's Len's part of the woods. And the girls' part of the woods. What's yours, Anne?"

"It's my tiny log house. It's just a little cottage, that's all. But I could live there my whole life. Nobody would ever come by. Well, you could, Alice, of course."

We leaned over the fence. There it was. Still.

"It's beautiful, Anne." Alice smiled. "We could take books there."

I showed her how to climb through the barbed-wire fence. We went up to it.

Its wood was no longer blond; it was gray like the stumps where Len had cut down the beetle trees. Its logs had big cracks along their length, because they were shrinking with time. Nails holding the logs together had become loose and were working their way out. If we got scratches from old barbed wire like we'd just gone through, or from rusted nails that stuck out, we could get tetanus.

The door to the little room was gone. What a loss, what an intrusion. But someone had leaned the door against the wall, on the outside. Oddly, the little house's window still had its glass. I looked inside. The cot was gone, along with its Indian blanket and kerosene lamp. The room was empty except for the little table, now on its side, and the forest debris—twigs, pine needles, and dead leaves among pools of dirt and dust on the wood floor. *Snow must blow in during the winter*, I thought. The floor would eventually buckle, rot. Then there would be birds' nests, insects. The log house was turning back into forest.

"I'm so sorry, Anne."

Silent, I turned back to the barbed-wire fence. She followed me.

Jane and Alan were already eating at the round table when we got back. They'd moved our possessions to the side. They smelled of marijuana, like that young man on El Camino Real who'd given me directions to Belmont.

Jane, then Alan, invited us to join them.

It turned out they were having ham sandwiches too, and beer. "No, I wouldn't like any beer," I said. After all, ladies didn't drink beer. In fact, I'd never tasted it. I got Alice and myself glasses of water.

"You should taste the mountain water," I said politely to Alan.

He looked surprised at my politeness. "Yes, I think I will."

So I got up and got him a big glass of my cold water. I got one for Jane too.

"Did you go walking?" I asked Jane, as Alan took big gulps, smiling with satisfaction.

"We went over to the cliffs, then along the road, then down to the spring. We took the little microscope to the spring, so Alan could look at the microbes. Alan's a scientist, you know. We had a wonderful time."

So here was Alan, seemingly at home in my other kitchen as well. He wasn't handsome. His skin was light brown, and he had a large, wide, flat nose. His wide forehead was slanted, pushing backward the hairline of his midnight-black hair. And he was rude; look at how he'd introduced himself to me back in Denver! But perhaps he was very intelligent. After all, he was Chinese. But he couldn't be as smart as my girls.

I'd forgotten to introduce him to Alice. I turned toward her, but she'd already begun to speak.

"I'm Alice Thatcher. I'm the Hopes' neighbor in Denver," she said, extending her hand.

Alan put down his sandwich, wiped his hands, and shook Alice's. She mentioned that she'd glimpsed him in the backyard, knew he and Jane had been in North Africa. "And were you in school before that?" she added.

"Yes, I was at UCLA."

"Oh, UCLA. You must be very intelligent. And the Peace Corps? Is there a story there?"

There was a story there, it turned out, and Alan didn't hesitate to tell it. He'd been getting his PhD. But the department had failed him on his comprehensive exams, then wouldn't let him retake them.

"I wasn't the right kind of person. I didn't fit their mold of what a PhD from UCLA should be like. I didn't fit their stereotype, that's all. In a nutshell."

He said that in earnestness, his face angry. Such a poor loser, so impressed with himself.

Jane, too, had a righteous look on her face. She was a little soldier marching beside him. Then I realized they were just that: righteous. Jane was still smoldering over her years of near-failing grades at Stanford, still smoldering over her rejection by that rich boy. Jane and Alan shared a world view, and it was not a pretty one—both in their mid-twenties and shot through with resentment.

They were staying over at the ranch for the night, then Alan was flying to his parents' home in California the next day.

"You're doing what? You are NOT spending the night together in any house of mine," I said.

Alan was silent.

Jane said evenly, "What difference does it make to you anyway?" She did not add "Mother."

"What will the neighbors say?" I let that sink in. Then I added, "What will your father say?"

Jane exchanged glances with Alan. "All right." She was angry. "We'll come back down."

When Alice and I left the cabin, it was the middle of the afternoon. I was embarrassed that she'd seen that exchange, and my mind was still on it, but Alice was looking around. As we were walking toward the car, she spotted, at the foot of a ponderosa tree, a large cocoon the color of ashes.

"Look, it must have come loose and fallen down," she said.

I picked the cocoon up off the ground and cradled it in my hand. It was so light. Ordinary enough, but delicate. And apparently alive inside.

"I'll bet it's a hawk moth. Those moths become as big as your hand," Alice said. "And they're gorgeous."

"Yes, I saw a picture once." I wrapped it in a tissue and carefully put it in the bottom of my purse.

I drove Alice and myself back down to Denver. Highway 285 was full of gentle, calming curves. At the bottom was Turkey Creek Canyon. The afternoon shadows, hundreds of feet deep, sculpted its steep granite walls. Even inside the car, we were warm in the direct sun and evening cool of the shadows. There was little traffic and it was moving slowly. Alice and I hadn't been talking, and I felt introspective. About the doomed cabin, about Jane. About that young man at my table. Then, about myself.

"Alice, did I ever tell you my parents were German immigrants?" I said impulsively, my eyes on the road. But I was tired of keeping it a secret.

"No, you did not."

She said it so matter-of-factly. How rare.

That moment, the sun shone through. I glanced over. There she was with her straw hat in her lap, her hands folded over its rim. A lady.

"You must be proud of them," she said. "Coming from so far away. Having to learn so much when they got here."

"They did learn a lot, even though they stayed in Germantown, in Akron. But life was hard for them sometimes. During World War I my father was paraded down a street and taunted because he was a Kaiser. But they raised five of us."

She bent toward me, and I glanced her way again. "Don't let it matter any longer. Don't let it."

I drove out of the canyon, my eyes on the road. Denver and the Eastern Plains stretched out before us.

That evening, in Denver, I put the cocoon in a small glass bowl and placed the bowl behind my kitchen sink, where it would be warm but not directly in the sun. I would guard it there, in its bowl, as it grew and changed right below its surface. One day it would burst forth, beautiful with its four huge brown-and-gray wings. Perhaps Leah would be home by then. I would give the big moth to her.

Turning, I saw my letter to Dr. Osborne on the dinette table. The letter I could never tell a single person about, because he and my own husband had accused and shamed me to the core. I tore it up and put it in the trash under the sink; I would not let that doctor read it and know the pain he'd caused me. Anyway, Alice would not have written that letter. She was a lady.

20

"Perhaps it's dead," I thought at the beginning of August. "Perhaps it was already dead when I picked it up from the ground by the ponderosa tree." I held the glass bowl that the cocoon was in up to my nose. It didn't smell of anything. I jiggled it a bit. Nothing looked different. "Maybe I should just throw it out."

Even the hot summer air was dead by two o'clock in the afternoon each day. I didn't see living things, like birds, through the picture window in the living room. Well, there were occasional butterflies—such delicate wings stirring up the dead air. Or maybe they didn't think it was dead. Maybe it was just me.

Maybe the air could no longer carry sound. That would account for the silence of my world.

So would the absence of people in it. Jane got up each day before I did, and quietly left for the campus in Boulder, in time for her eight o'clock class. When she got home in the afternoon, she smiled in my direction, on her way to her room to study. All this so she could get her grade average up, to be admitted to the University of Minnesota, where Alan would be making a second effort at getting a PhD. If all went well, Jane would be studying for a master's in library science.

Jane, a librarian, I thought. That sounded just like her, prim and proper and methodical.

Len was seldom around as well. Ever since the morning he'd accused me of not having a heart condition, he'd kept his distance. Clearly, he'd made some decision about me, and that was that. Just like Jane must have done, at the beginning of the summer.

But there was another reason Len was keeping his distance; he was hiding from me. The morning of the accusation, he'd stood up to me, attacked me, left me speechless. He'd never systematically confronted me like that before, sure of himself, going for the kill. Well, he'd sometimes lost his temper with me—most recently when he'd wanted to hit me but had instead slammed the big lamp down at the motel on El Camino Real. But this time, here in my dinette while I was eating breakfast, he'd set a precedent; this Len was strong, in control, certain.

Now the fact of the matter was, he could never measure up to that again. He knew it, and so did I. And he certainly couldn't measure up to it with Johnny Scannell. Len's pursed lips and rigidly held neck announced as he came home from work that this was the summer of just-bearable tension between them. After a quickly eaten dinner, Len would go do repairs on washing machines and dryers, his teeth grinding as he surely thought, *Johnny Scannell ... Johnny Scannell*, with each turn of a screw or a bolt.

Back home again, before bed, he would sit on the back patio with his cigar and his daughter. In their wicker chairs, in the dark, Len and Jane were mostly silent, or spoke in low voices. Jane caught me watching once. She slightly raised the corner of her mouth. Then she turned back to him. I returned to my kitchen. My silence was broken by the voice of a Siamese cat, a rasp against the dead air.

A week before Jane finished up her schoolwork in Boulder and was to go to Minneapolis, the ash-colored cocoon moved. I saw it when I went to rinse my plate after my noontime sandwich. Perhaps it had been moving all morning. I took the cocoon in its glass bowl to the dinette table and sat down to watch the birth.

The moth emerged headfirst, and then came its thorax, legs, wings, and abdomen. It was all dark at first: an inch-and-a-half long. I could see that it needed to dry off. Gradually, the moth spread out its wings. It stood on its six legs and shivered the wings for perhaps half an hour, to dry them. They became beautiful—dull brown with lines of deep gray. Bits of pink edged the back wings. The moth had a pink-and-gray spotted abdomen.

I let it stand on my yellow placemat to dry off and become fuzzy, fully a moth. I left to dust the living room, straighten the furniture out in the back, empty the waste baskets. Then I took a shower, thinking now and then about where I would keep the moth until Leah got here. When I had put on fresh clothes and combed my hair, I went back to the kitchen, eager to see what the moth was looking like now.

Leah's hideous cat, up on the table, was chewing hard on the moth's thorax. He had discarded its wings, which were lying askew on the placemat.

It was still alive, so I yelled the cat away and killed what was left of the moth with the head of a spoon.

Jane had been watching this from the kitchen. She stepped forward to the dinette, her eyebrows raised.

"You killed it. You are unspeakably cruel." She sputtered for words.

I pushed my chair back in. "It's an insect. They can't feel anything."

Fury on her face. "That's the way you are with every one of us. Look at me. You've always assumed I don't have any feelings. From as early as I can remember."

Jane picked up the books she'd put down on the kitchen counter and marched toward the hall. But she stopped and turned back. "And you treated Alan terribly. I brought my future husband home, and you sidestepped him every chance you got. Alan in one room, you in another, all day long. How do you think that made me feel, my mother rejecting the man I'm going to marry? And it's all because he's Chinese, isn't it? Admit it. It's all because he's Chinese."

By now, deep shadows were falling across the dinette and kitchen. I felt cold.

"Admit it."

"Jane, I am not prejudiced. I am not prejudiced against anyone. I would invite anyone into my home. Gladly. But that Alan you brought home is rude, and he's arrogant." I tried to sound gentle. "He's not our type, Jane. You'd be better off without him."

She cocked her head. Her cheeks were blotched with red. "Yes. All alone. I would definitely be better off all alone."

"Yes, Jane, you would. You're beautiful and intelligent and a Stanford graduate."

"If I'd never set foot in Stanford, I would have been a lot happier."

"It's your fault you never took advantage of Stanford."

"I tried my best. I tried my very best. But you neve cared about what I was going through, what it did to me. All you cared about was Leah and all her straight As."

Her chin raised, she paused in thought for a moment. "Well, guess what, you're going to have to live with Alan from here on out, because we're going to get married at Christmas time. You'll just have to eat your prejudices and stand there and watch it happen, because it's going to happen. At Christmas break."

"All right, if you hate me that much, I won't go and spoil it for you."

After the moth argument, Jane and I walked around each other like noiseless robots for days. Jane and Len, the two conspirators, had arranged for her to leave at an hour when he could drive her to the airport. She and I nodded at each other early that morning as she negotiated the front door with two big suitcases containing the entirety of her possessions, except for her Stanford textbooks. Clearly, she had no intention of ever coming back.

Oddly, I wanted to go to her room. There, I found perfume in the air. I imagined it floating on atoms of Jane, which lingered in the room, slowly settling on her everyday objects. She could be such a little girl. Both of my daughters could be.

As for myself, I never was one, but what could you expect of a girl who was the oldest of five children of German immigrants, who spoke almost no English? When I was growing up, I just took care of others, plain and simple. I was a sort of head of the household, taking children to doctors, parents to doctors, children to school, explaining to others what my parents—lacking their own words—wanted.

I hadn't thought of that for years, decades.

Really, though, there was nothing to think of; I just never was a little girl.

Looking out Jane's window at the bounty of well-tended lawns and large houses, I examined vague memories of having to stand when Pop entered the room, of having to eat our meals at the big wooden table without speaking, of not being allowed to take exercise class at school because Pop thought bloomers for girls were indecent. Our family portrait: all of us girls in black dresses with little white collars which Mom had crocheted, not a smile on any of our faces.

I sat down on Jane's bed. She'd folded the blanket and stripped the sheets and pillowcases; of course Jane would leave on a note of neatness. In that way, she was a true Kaiser.

Somehow, that made me think about Claire Dougherty. Claire from the BF Goodrich Tire and Rubber Factory, who slept in a yellow bedroom in Germantown and had a big white hat and blonde hair; everything about her was beautiful, and she laughed. Surely she was still alive, back in Ohio. With a smile like hers, she must have married rich, had lots of children. Boys. Boys who laughed.

Later, I heard Len drive up into the garage. He came in through the back door, by the dinette.

"Well, she got off just fine," he said.

"I hope she has a good trip," I said.

"Well. I think she'll be all right now."

"What do you mean, 'now'?"

"We talked about Alan on the way to the airport. She wanted my blessing. I told her, 'I'd rather Alan wasn't Chinese, but that's what he is, and that's the way it is. So you have my blessing.'"

"You must be very proud of yourself."

He didn't appear to notice my tone. A little smile of self-satisfaction on his face. "Yes. I guess I am."

It was midmorning, and the dinette was toasty from the sun. I put fresh coffee in my mug and sat back to look out the window. I didn't know where Len had gone. Probably off to collect money or fix machines. I didn't care. I felt almost lazy.

Alice was coming across the lawn to my front door. A blonde girl was with her. I hurried to the door.

"Anne, this is my daughter, Susan. She's home. I just had to show my beautiful Susan to you."

Susan stepped forward to me and, with an enthusiastic smile, extended her hand. Then she impulsively hugged me. "Mother has told me so much about you."

Her blonde hair hung around her shoulders. She brushed it to her back, but it fell down on her shoulders again.

Claire.

I stood back, held her hands, and said, "Susan. I finally get to meet Susan."

She blushed, puckered her smiling lips, and held her head high.

"Oh, Alice, you and Susan come in and have a cup of coffee," I said.

"Of course," Alice said, and we went inside to my table. "This nook is so sunny. I love the end of August. Susan and I are going to lunch at Hummel's, the one in Cherry Creek.

We're celebrating; Susan's enrolled in Loretto Heights College. Classes start in two weeks."

"Oh my. What are you going to study?"

"Art. I want to be an art teacher," said Susan.

"She'll be in school again—full-time—and living at home," said Alice. "We're proud, Susan."

Mother and daughter smiled at each other.

21

Len said Leah might be phoning us one of these days.
And she did.
"Mother, it's me."
I had that feeling you get when bells were ringing above you. My wonderful daughter. She was the bells ringing; she always had been. Leah prancing. Joy.
"Mother, I miss you." Brave words from my young girl.
"Oh, honey, I've missed you so much."
"Mother, I want to come home."
Her voice was the oddest combination of young woman and old woman. But at least she didn't sound like the hollow-voiced child she'd been that night she had called home three months before, at the beginning of the ordeal.
Now we were at the end. My daughter was coming home in time for fall, just around the corner, accompanying the shedding of old, useless, unwanted leaves. Everything in the world would then rest for a while.

They wouldn't be letting her come home if she wasn't well, would they?

"I want to see my cat, Morgan."

All right, she was only twenty-one. Her cat—apparently his name was Morgan—was a big deal to her. And she'd had the courage to call me, the mother she'd been so angry at. Where had her anger gone? Maybe they'd drawn it out of her, like pus out of a wound, in that big white showboat nightmare of mine. Maybe she was leaving *her* nightmare behind there. But mine persisted, of being stoned in a public place by those know-it-all people. The one —that woman—I still angered at.

Stop it, I said to myself.

But my mind kept picking at it. Whose anger was greater, Leah's at the hospital, or mine here? I realized I was the only one who could think to ask that. Yeah, stupid Anne indeed.

Still, I wanted to ask if Leah was still mad at me. If she still felt I had harmed her so badly. If I was still guilty. Only she could answer.

I hated that. I wondered if she knew the power she held. And here she was, coming home.

"Mother, I'm calling from my psychiatrist's office. He's cool."

The first call to her mother, and, wouldn't you know it, observed by one of those doctors. They would discuss and analyze it after she hung up.

I was a scarecrow tied to a barbed wire fence that nasty boys were throwing pellets at, laughing, outdoing each other.

Len brought Leah home from the airport. I was glad for that. I had wanted to stay home, so I could grasp her, hug her privately, welcome her into the house, the kitchen, her room.

Us, no bustling airport strangers to distract us, derail us. It was a matter of welcoming my girl into my arms more than it was a matter of territory. But it was that too. My territory, not that of the doctors or Mrs. Hunter.

Leah arrived in time for dinner. I gasped as I opened the front door to her; she was wearing blue jeans and her gray "J.S. Bach" t-shirt. Right where she'd left off with us.

But she'd dyed her hair blonde. "They encouraged self-expression," she laughed, "and I always wanted to be blonde." No amount of hair dye could make black hair into blonde. It was a blackish sort of orange. It wasn't just brassy; it was orange, with black roots.

Who ... *what* was my daughter?

Len said, kind of like an orator, "We're glad to have Leah home. Since it's Thursday, we won't start thinking about a job for her until next week. That way she can have a few days to rest up from her trip."

At dinner, macaroni and cheese, her favorite.

I asked her how her flight was. I pointed out the beginning of fall colors on the trees. Then there would be snow. Would she like to try skiing this year?

Leah observed it was so quiet here, something she found weird after all the noise of the hospital. She said the word. Hospital.

"Would you like us to rent you a piano? You could take lessons. You've always wanted to. That way we could have music in the house," I said. "It wouldn't seem so quiet."

How do you ask a girl who's just been in a mental hospital how she's feeling?

I didn't.

After she'd gone to bed, Len and I sat in the living room, he in his cobalt-blue leather chair and I by the afghan on the sofa. The cat wandered by. It hadn't seemed to notice Leah, and she'd forgotten to greet it earlier.

"She seems like her old self again," Len said.

"It's all been so sudden. But I'm glad to have her back home. What did her doctor tell you when she was discharged?"

"Her doctor said she was going to be okay. He gave her a bottle of pills. When they're all gone, I bet she'll be okay," he said. "Make sure she takes them."

"How am I supposed to say that to her?"

"Well, I don't know. You'll figure it out. But things aren't so bad, are they? She'll be fine after she gets a job and settles in."

"Maybe she shouldn't get a job right away. Maybe she wants to rest for a while. Maybe she doesn't want to work yet."

"Well, she should work. And she wants to. She told me so."

"When did she tell you that?"

Len thought for a moment. The cat jumped on his lap. He absently stroked it, then shooed it off. "Well, when I went out to visit her last month, I took her to the United plant by the airport. I thought she could find something to do there, a job like you had when you started out at BF Goodrich. The United plant is a big operation. They were working on three DC-8s when we were there, all in assembly lines. Leah said she was frightened. She wanted to leave right away. 'All right, maybe it's not the right job,' I said, 'but we'll find you the right job.' She nodded. She wants to work, I know that."

I shuddered at his stupidity. "Len, give her a little time."

"I'll give her a week."

At about ten the next morning, in a t-shirt featuring "The Grateful Dead," Leah slid into a dinette chair and put a large bottle of large blue pills on the table. "I'm supposed to take these."

"What are they?"

"It says 'Stelazine.'"

"What are you supposed to do when you run out?"

"Go to a shrink and get some more, I guess. But I'm not going to a shrink. I'm well now."

"Oh." I just stared at her. What on earth could I, the culprit after all, say to that?

"Do you like my Grateful Dead t-shirt? They're big now. Before they got big, they used to play Saturday nights at the student union. Robin and I would go dance to their music."

"Where do you suppose Robin Pierpoint III is now?"

"Mo-ther! Don't call him that, like you were impressed by him or something. He was a phony. He's just gone."

Leah went over to the stove and helped herself to a bowl of oatmeal, filling it nearly to the top.

Should I notice she'd gained all that weight back, or should I say nothing?

"Did Morgan sleep with you last night?" I asked.

"No. He doesn't recognize me. My heart's broken."

I drove her down to south Broadway, to Joe Onofrio's Piano Company. I'd never known anybody who'd had any kind of piano, big or small. I imagined Len hadn't either. Well, maybe Virginia Gunderson's mansion had a piano, a big black one, back in Oak Park. I wondered idly who lived in that mansion now. Or maybe she was still there, drinking sherry and becoming old. Did Virginia know how to play a musical instrument? Well, my pop could play the violin. He'd even had one. I wondered whose attic it was in now.

We arranged to rent a brand-new, cherry-brown upright piano, and then we went back home. There Leah slipped over into her other mind, the one of the illness, which I was still blamed for. She carried her stereo and all her records up from the basement, where I'd stored her California belongings when I had them shipped back.

After helping herself to leftover macaroni and cheese, Leah went back to her room and closed the door. In a minute, rock music with irritating, primitive beats took over the house.

This continued. At about two o'clock, I knocked on her door, to ask her to turn it down; the Thatchers might hear it and get annoyed. Maybe Susan didn't listen to that kind of music—not all young people did. Anyway, Susan was busy studying.

Leah's music was so loud that she didn't hear me knock. I knocked twice more, then opened the door a crack.

"Mo-ther, knock first!"

I looked in. She was sitting in her upholstered chair. She bent over and lifted the stylus off the record.

"May I?" I sat down on the edge of her bed. She looked worn out from all that driving intensity. "Leah— "

"Don't you just love the Doors? That was 'Journey to the End of the Night.'"

Perhaps that was *my* song. Yes, that was a corny thought.

But I couldn't wait any longer. I blurted, "Oh, Leah, do you still blame me? I feel so guilty."

She looked me right in the eye, took a deep breath, and

hissed slowly, "You're a terrible mother. I just want you out of my head."

She turned away, red faced. Her eyes were brilliant.

I got my coat and purse and the bottle of blue pills and went to my car. I drove over to the university hospital, which was only a mile from Crestmoor Park. After I parked on the street, I asked a couple of students where the psychiatric professors were. They pointed to a large white building down the street. When I got close to it, I saw that "PSYCHIATRY" was written across the top in huge letters.

I was scared. I went in.

Down a broad hall and to the left were a large waiting room and elevators. At the far end of the hall, a sign read "Chairman of Psychiatry."

A minute later, I asked his secretary if I might speak to him.

She tilted her head.

"I need to know what this bottle of pills is for," I explained.

She asked me if she might see it. She looked at it, and then went and knocked on the professor's inner door. After a moment she came back. "He can see you for a moment."

I went in there. He was an older man with a clipped, silver mustache. How he looked like Dr. Osborne! Loneliness welled in me like an orphan, loneliness and anger. But this man was wearing a regular street suit, with a striped-blue tie. He had a big, paper-stacked desk with leather chairs behind and in front of it. There was a framed poster from a psychiatric conference in Vienna, a burgundy carpet, a big window, and in front of the window, a small table with two small chairs.

He asked me to sit opposite him at the big desk. "My secretary said you're Mrs. Hope. And you've come about this bottle of pills?"

"Yes."

"Well, I have a few minutes before my next meeting, and I'll be glad to answer a question or two."

That was reassuring, like I'd made the right decision in coming here. He was clearly not at all like Dr. Pauley at Stanford. I found myself blurting, "My daughter just got out of a mental sanitarium. They gave her those to take with her. The doctors never told us what was wrong with her, except that she had a nervous breakdown. She blames me. They all blame me, the doctors, my family. They all blame me."

Oh—I had just offloaded to a complete stranger. Because there was nobody else, and after all, here I was at the end of my rope.

The doctor twiddled a pencil back and forth between his thumb and his forefinger. Then I realized he was holding his chin in. Looking down at me. "Stelazine is usually used to treat schizophrenia. I'm surprised they didn't give you a diagnosis. But perhaps at the time you were, understandably, so distraught that—"

"I was not!"

He looked surprised at me.

What could that grotesqueness—that *schizophrenia*—have to do with Leah? It couldn't be true. I was confused and didn't know what question to ask first. "What causes schizophrenia?"

He replied slowly. "It's almost invariably caused by the mother. We call her a schizophrenogenic mother."

"Why? I love my daughter."

"The schizophrenogenic mother both loves and hates her child, simultaneously."

They were all around me. California, now here.

"Would you write that word down for me, please?" I asked.

"Certainly." He produced a prescription pad from his pile of papers and wrote it out. He tore the prescription off the pad and reached across his desk to hand it to me. He'd carefully written the word out in all capital letters, so there was no doubt about it. "Have you considered psychiatric help for yourself, Mrs. Hope?"

"May I please have the bottle of pills back?"

I took the prescription and the pills and stood up. I didn't shake his hand. He didn't offer his. He remained behind his desk.

His secretary knocked and then peered in to remind him of his meeting.

The prescription folded away inside my wallet, the bottle of pills put back in the dinette, I went about setting the table when I got home. We would have rib eye steak, mashed potatoes, and green beans: all so normal, so ordinary, so everyday. Every family in America. I was shaking again.

But first I went to check on my daughter. Her door was wide open, the way I'd left it. Some woman was yelling on the stereo.

Leah acted like nothing had happened at all. "That's Janis Joplin. She died last year. She was just twenty-seven. Drug overdose. Isn't that sad?"

22

Len spent Saturday fixing washers and dryers at his little warehouse space out east, on the other side of Stapleton Airport. I imagined the scene. His two part-time workers would be there with him; the three of them good at what they did, listening to sports and talk-radio as they repaired machines, talking working-man talk, making working-man jokes. How he must have resented fat Johnny Scannell then.

When Len had finished his day and came home to dinner, he was surprised by the brand-new cherry-brown piano. It stood against the wall in the little alcove between the front door and the living room.

"That's a beautiful machine," Len said to Leah and me, grinning, his eyebrows raised. "Well, a beautiful instrument, I guess you would say."

"See that bench; I can store my music inside," said Leah.

Standing back from it, Len looked the whole thing over carefully. "I want to go scrub my hands."

He turned to walk toward the bathroom, then turned back. He had a twinkle in his eye when he said to me, "You know, this house would look classy with its own piano. It would be an investment. I wonder how much they ask for one of these."

That evening I called Alice over to look at it. It was nice to see a piano in a house, she had said. How she missed theirs. They'd had a piano for Susan in Jakarta, and she'd loved it, but had nowhere to play now, which was a shame.

"Then Susan and Leah should share this piano," I said. "Susan can come over whenever she wants for study breaks, or during the evening."

"And Susan can practice teaching. Leah will be her first student. They can pretend that it's a school for piano playing."

Leah appeared from her room. "Oh, let's do that! I'm stoked."

Alice and I took the two girls over to the branch library in Cherry Creek on Sunday morning. Leah and Susan liked each other immediately. My daughter was in awe of Susan's long blonde hair, and Susan wanted to hear all about California. Alice and Susan got Leah *The Student's Introduction to the Piano*.

"Look," Susan said, "in no time at all—maybe a week—you'll be playing 'Au Clair de la Lune' and 'Chopsticks.'"

"Wow. That is so cool."

Susan spent much of the afternoon with Leah in our "piano alcove." From time to time, I walked by and listened to them talking.

"Finger exercises are what you'll do today," said Susan, after explaining the various notes and sharps and flats.

"I am totally impressed. I mean, you are awesome."

"Now, if you want to be a serious pianist, you should look professional. How about your hair? I think it should be more natural."

"Do you think? Hmmm."

After Susan left, Leah practiced. She practiced and practiced. Leah knew no fatigue until she was hollow.

Len, when he got home from the warehouse, put up with about half an hour of the finger exercises. "I think you've played about enough for today, Leah."

"No, I haven't. I'm just getting good. I'll be really good by the time I go to bed tonight."

"You'll stop NOW."

Dinner averted a fight between them. But Leah talked piano all through dinner. Len's forehead became wrinkled, weary of it.

I was clearing the table, about to wash the dishes, when Susan knocked at the front door. Charles and Alice were with her.

"Can I play just a piece or two for my parents?" Susan held up her sheet music, clearly dear to her. "I brought it all the way from Jakarta."

Two girls and four parents and a classical music recital. We sat in the living room—Len the host in his leather chair, the one thing he'd had me buy when we moved to Crestmoor Park—and watched and listened to Susan in the alcove. Neither Len nor I recognized the names of the composers, except Beethoven. Beethoven in our living room! Len's crinkled smile of satisfaction —I knew he would go ahead and buy the piano. We would become completely upper-middle class, and we'd be a happy, peaceful family again. Someday, somehow, even Jane would join us, and we might frame a drawing of hers for the living room wall, above the sofa.

The next morning, having apparently taken Susan's advice, Leah went to the store and got herself some dark-brown Lady Clairol hair color. After an hour in the bathroom, she looked like—well, I breathed a sigh of relief. Another little bit of her was back to normal.

When he got home from work, Len looked her over and said, "Fine. Now you can go get yourself a job, like you're supposed to."

On the other hand, Jane—oh, his Jane! She called once a week or so from Minnesota. One Friday evening, Len and I had just finished dinner. He was sitting with his tea while I was clearing the table when the phone rang. Jane's voice was prim and proper. She didn't even ask how I was. I passed the phone to her father. He hunched over with the receiver, his face now down, concentrating, hanging onto her every word. A whole world, just the two of them. I watched from the sink.

In the background, Leah was struggling at "Au Clair de la Lune."

Then Leah, yielding to the annoyance of her father's anger, arranged an appointment with the Empire Employment Agency downtown. She smiled at me like it was going to be a lot of fun. "Just think, they're going to find me a job as a prima ballerina in New York City."

"That's not funny. What about your father?" I asked. "He's got enough problems right now without your attitude."

In her enthusiasm, Leah called Susan—who had no classes that day. They planned to go downtown on one of Denver's brand-new, huge buses. They'd start with the employment agency, and then have lunch at the elegant restaurant on the fifth floor of the Denver Dry Goods Company, the city's landmark clothing store.

"We'll have Monte Carlo sandwiches," Leah said to me. "We'll be just like those rich ladies out shopping downtown."

Something dreadful happened in the restaurant.

Leah came home, midafternoon, with fury in her eyes. She wouldn't talk, except to say that she was angry. She went into her room and shut the door.

An hour later, Alice, in a too-quiet voice, asked me to come over. Susan, still all dressed up, was sitting in their dinette. She'd been crying.

"Susan, what happened?" I asked, bending over her.

She started crying again.

"Susan, did Leah do something to you?"

She bent over and put her head in her arms for a moment. Then she straightened and looked at her mother for comfort. "I just didn't know she was going to do that."

"Do what?" I said in alarm.

"Start yelling at the headwaiter because he put his arm around her waist and called her a 'dear young thing,' or something like that."

Susan wasn't embarrassed. She was frightened. By my daughter.

"Leah yelled at him to get his hand off of her," she continued. "She called him macho. And a dirty old man. And a male chauvinist pig. Loud. Everyone stared at us, all the ladies having their lunch. I could have just died. I wanted out. The manager—in a suit like Father's—came over and asked us to leave. I ran out of the restaurant, out of Denver Dry. People on the street looked at me because I was going along crying. I came straight home."

Susan asked her mother if she could go to her room. Alice looked bewildered and worried.

"Maybe we ought to stop the piano lessons." That was all I could think of to say, when Susan was gone.

"Let's do that, for a while. Remember, Susan's had her share of emotional problems in the past, too. I know she's over-reacting ..."

"Alice, I am so, so sorry. Let me go in and apologize to Susan."

"No, let's just let Susan be alone for the rest of the day."

I wasn't exactly *mad* at Leah, though. I was disturbed. Now a public outburst in downtown, and I was helpless.

I sat down in the living room, by my afghan. I suddenly thought of a book—a popular book back then—that I read when Leah was tiny and howling day and night, nothing but a hopeless, wrinkled-up, red face that responded to no one: *The Bad Seed.*

I could remember only once in Leah's life that she had ever been kind to me; she'd comforted me when Virginia Gunderson had abandoned me and my new engagement ring, there in my kitchen at the ranch. Leah would have been about fifteen or sixteen. Only once in her life.

Leah had never, as far as I knew, been kind to Jane. Or to her father. To tell the truth, not to her father at all. Now, Susan.

The Bad Seed.

What would be coming next?

Len was so angry at Johnny Scannell that evening that I let go of the whole business of Leah's outburst and Susan. Like it had never happened, as far as he knew.

I heard Leah come out of her room and get herself some food from the refrigerator after we'd gone to bed.

In the middle of the next Friday morning, Leah got a phone call from the Empire Employment Agency. A financial company on 17th Street was looking for a young woman who'd graduated from an eastern women's college. Stanford would be just as welcome, the company had said. Could Leah make a two o'clock interview?

Leah jumped with excitement in the middle of my kitchen. "My ship is coming in. Father will now get off my back."

"All right, you've got two hours to get ready. Then you should take a cab so you'll look fresh. I'll give you some money."

I beamed at her enthusiasm. After all was said and done, Leah's enthusiasm—when it was there—was the most joyful thing I'd ever known. "Do you have your resume?"

"God—I left it with those guys at the Empire Employment Agency."

"Well, you'll have to swing by and pick it up. And don't say 'God,' and don't say 'guy.' These bankers are looking for a young woman with elite manners."

"It's *eh*-leet, Mother, not *ee*-leet."

She skipped off to her room like a child.

About six o'clock, when Len was in his blue chair and nursing not only his drink but also his bruised feelings from a day with Charlie Scannell, Leah came in the front door. She was crying.

What was wrong?

Her father looked directly upon her tears with his defeated face. Each seemed to realize the other one was worse off.

"I went for a job interview," Leah told her father, after she blew her nose. "With some bankers on 17th Street. They wanted a young woman from an eastern college, or Stanford."

Len's face was exhausted and intrigued at the same time.

"They wanted a GIRL all dressed up chic," she said, "with her fancy degree and superior mind, to POINT WITH A STICK at figures on a board at meetings."

That anyone could do that to my brilliant daughter. Len looked bilious.

"So I pulled my resume out of that banker's hand, or whoever he was, and walked right out."

The now-curling resume lay on top of her purse, which she'd discarded on the floor.

The cat wreathed her ankles, loud. Morgan and the rumpled tissue Leah held—and that resume—were all she really had in this world.

Len said faintly, his face screwed up, "Well, maybe you should have just taken the job. Maybe they would have gotten to know you and given you something better as time went on."

Leah turned in fury on him, picked up her purse, and shouted at both of us, but especially at Len, "I hate you, I really hate you."

I would have taken Len's hand, both his hands, but … but what? I didn't know how.

The next day, Len was already gone to his warehouse unit when Leah appeared in the kitchen. Still in her nightgown, hair uncombed, she drank coffee and ate toast.

She swallowed the wrong way on crumbs, and coughing and coughing, she began to cry. I could tell it was a general sort of cry, about everything.

I looked at her eyes, closed, tears escaping. "You did the right thing yesterday, walking out. I'm proud of you."

"Somebody in the house proud of me—that's a joke," she yelled.

Feeling futile, I got up and went to put plates and utensils away. We were like drops of water on a hot iron, skittering frantically away from each other.

Thatchers. What happened when one of them reached out to another? Did Susan shout at them, at their kindnesses?

And, right then, Susan was at our door.

Leah let her in. They talked quietly in the hall.

"Susan and I are going to go walk around Crestmoor Park. I've got to change first, and comb my hair."

It was touching to see how glad Leah was to see her.

Standing there, Susan looked vulnerable, brave. She'd done the right thing, had taken a risk for someone she cared about. I realized then that Susan would be all right for the rest of her life.

Would Leah be all right too? It was anybody's guess. Right now, I hoped for the peace of one afternoon. I gave Leah ten dollars, to take Susan to lunch at The Bagel after their walk.

When the girls returned, they were friends again. Just like that, beautiful together again. Even Leah was capable of making up, continuing what mattered. So I had, for a weird, incongruous moment, the notion that at some point I must have done something or other right in raising my daughter. Well, I didn't know what, except for the horses and the other gifts for growing up. But perhaps something more? Something that would save the day?

They played piano for the rest of the afternoon. At one point, I went from the kitchen to the alcove to watch and listen. It was Susan's turn. "I'm going to play Beethoven, since you like his music, Mrs. Hope. This is 'Ode to Joy,'" she said.

Afterward, we were all silent, since it had been so beautiful. "Now," said Susan, "I'm going to teach Leah how to play the version in her student book."

I continued to giddily fantasize about the old Leah. Of course she was capable of joy. She was the daughter who had accumulated language after language, beauty everywhere she opened a book. And she projected beauty and joy, at least to me. At least, in this very moment.

That evening, after Len had smoked his cigar on the back patio, Leah played "Ode to Joy" for him. It was our first recital. Then Leah left us alone in the living room and went out by herself to the dark in the backyard. Maybe she was a little girl again looking at the stars. Len and I sat almost in darkness ourselves. Only the hall light was on.

23

Sunday afternoon, the Thatchers were having a cocktail party. I sat down at my vanity, in my bra, girdle, half-slip, and nylons. I honestly didn't know why I had a vanity, except that it and its matching little brocaded seat were necessary pieces of furniture in a nice bedroom. It matched the two mahogany beds. I'd bought them all at once, because I disliked shopping, in particular around salesmen who knew more than I did and let me know that by peering down their noses at me.

My first cocktail party. I looked in the mirror. I realized I hadn't looked in that vanity mirror since I'd been back from California. I stared at myself—the same small face, big nose, too-big eyes, thin lips. Mrs. Hunter appeared in my imagination: younger than I was by a decade, rounded face with pink cheeks, a strong but straight nose, full and firm lips. I had been the deer in her headlights.

Today I was going to wear my pink rhinestone necklace and earrings with my favorite dress—the navy-blue one. My parents had given me this, my first real jewelry, when I graduated high school back in Akron. It had the best-quality rhinestones, mounted in shiny stainless steel. Lots of people didn't even go to high school in those days. Graduation was a big honor. My parents were so proud of me.

I thought then of my mother. I was her first child, born when she was eighteen. My sister, Betty, said that Mother was illiterate. I guess I didn't know that, because I really didn't know who she was—Mother, I meant. Oh yes, I remembered her Christmas tree each year, with real, lit candles. And I remembered the big meals for seven that she made, and the occasional pastries. Hearing her whistling as she went about her day. She'd had a heart condition, and eventually died of it. *"A heart condition"—words I'm not allowed to use now*, I thought angrily. Anyway, Mother had told Betty she hadn't wanted to be buried in black, so she was buried in a blue dress. I wondered, startling myself for a moment, if it was the same color as the dress I would wear today.

Just now Len needed me. He came up by the vanity and said, "Dammit, I don't know what to wear to an afternoon party in somebody's house." Well, I didn't know what he should wear either. He had suits and mechanic overalls and one pair of jeans, and that was about it. Then he said, "I'll wear my best suit, because it's Charles' party."

A real party—yes, it was a milestone. A sort of second graduation. Now I truly belonged in Crestmoor Park. And I could, if bored, change the subject from Oak Park and Virginia Gunderson's cocktail party if I ever saw *her* again.

But in a practical way, I was filled with little fears. What would be served? How long should we stay? What should we do when we got there? Most importantly, would Len make faux pas? But Leah would be going with us. We could take cues from our sophisticated daughter. I reminded Len of that, and he said that was nonsense: "We'll be just fine!"

Leah said we shouldn't go over exactly when the party would be starting, because that was "so gauche, *so* gauche."

Len said, "The party starts at three, and we'll be there at three."

As a result, we were the first ones there. Alice—who was wearing paisley silk trousers with bell bottoms and a beige silk blouse—came to me, took me by the hand, and said, "Anne, you're my best friend, and I couldn't be happier that you're starting our party."

She was making tiny adjustments to the food as the caterers were leaving through the back. Charles was making little adjustments to the variously shaped glasses and bottles.

Susan and Leah found each other right away. Both in their best pantsuits, they went out back to talk and to see the dogs, and then Susan came back to help her mother. Leah stood with Len.

Soon there were four middle-aged couples, then eight, then Susan put some jazz piano music on the stereo, as a soft background.

I stood by the table with the appetizers, because I didn't know where else to go. Then women came up to me and introduced themselves; I was so tickled, full of (almost) joy. Leah's kind of joy.

Leah—where was she? While I was talking with the women, I watched her. She was moving slowly around the room, holding a glass of what must have been Coke, talking to both men and women twice or three times her age, a lovely smile on her face, elegant like Jackie Kennedy, with the same dark hair. My daughter was a lady indeed, a lady who'd been to college. I was so proud of her. I looked to see if Len was noticing her too. He was deeply into a conversation, smiling his crinkled smile, head tossed back. Scotch in hand, he seemed in the middle of impressing and being impressed.

Other men wore suits, too, so I was relieved. But some men wore handsome sweaters. Len had never had a sweater. Perhaps I would get him one to wear around Charles.

None of the other women worked either. They talked to me about their husbands' work, their own volunteering, children and grandchildren, travel trips. I surprised myself by talking with them, adding to the conversation. And I said I would volunteer as soon as my younger daughter had left home. I pointed her out, and the other women smiled as they glimpsed her being so charming.

A particular woman intrigued me. She and her husband had just been to Germany. She described the rich, green countryside, the recklessly fast autobahns, the little towns with their cheerful restaurants that all served schnitzel and pastries. Munich, the famous clock towers in the middle of towns that you would see in pictures, and the beer halls: "Imagine me in a beer hall," the woman exclaimed.

I was won over by her enthusiasm for the place I'd always been ashamed of, and I found myself saying, "Well, my parents were from—"

Shrieking. My daughter's shrieking voice. I was confused, immediately thinking she was hurt. Then I heard her words. I was mortified.

"Goddamn it, I am not a goldbricker! I worked as hard at Stanford as you ever did with your old washing machines."

The room fell silent, everyone staring at Leah.

She was standing in front of her father, whose face was shocked, then furious.

"All you and Mother ever do is put me down. That's all you ever do!" Leah yelled at Len. "Over and over, how much trouble I've caused you. Let me tell you, I wish Charles Thatcher was my father."

She threw her Coke down onto the beige carpet. As though in a dream, I noticed gratefully that the glass wasn't broken.

"That's enough, that's enough," Len whispered loudly, seizing her by the arm. He pushed her through the crowd to the back door, and then out. People looked.

My mouth wide open, my cheeks hot, I whispered, "Alice, oh Alice, I'm so sorry."

Alice took both of my hands and kissed my cheek. "You go help Len now. We'll be just fine here."

"I put her in her room," Len said when I saw him over in our hall. He looked like he'd been slapped hard, had almost lost his balance.

We both sat down in the living room to catch our breaths.

He put his head back on his blue chair. "I can't go on like this."

"I can't either."

But we had no way out, did we?

"If I had any idea what to do …" Len trailed off.

"Call your doctor tomorrow," I said. "He'll know what to do."

I squeezed my eyes shut and forced a big tear out. Maybe that was trite, but it was a real tear. It skidded down my cheek.

"Well, that's not going to do you any good," Len said.

I'd decided what I would do long before getting up the next morning.

I didn't tell Len; he hadn't slept well, if he'd slept at all. I'd woken up at about four o'clock, and he was not in his bed. I'd waited for him to come back, and then I got up and found him in his chair. He was staring straight ahead, the cat there.

"Come to bed, Len. You have to work tomorrow."

He didn't answer.

Sunrise would start in an hour or so. I turned back to the bedroom.

"I want some bacon and eggs today," he said when I got up. "I need some strength." He was pale, almost gray, and his hands shook.

After he'd left for United, I got dressed. I was almost out the door. Then I thought, *Leah*, and went to her room. There was no sound inside. I opened her door a crack. She was sound asleep. Beside her, on the floor, was a box of Cheerios which she must have taken from the kitchen at some point during the night.

I went to my credit union, where I'd kept the five-thousand dollars that I'd made Len give me, so I could have some freedom. Then I drove around aimlessly. I almost went up to the ranch just for the comforting scenery, to watch the aspens, now yellow. But I was hungry, so I stopped at Hummel's for a corned beef sandwich. I drove more after that, back toward our old house on Bellaire Street. Suddenly, I found myself turning back and ending up at the public library in Cherry Creek. I went in and asked the librarian at the desk for an easy-to-understand book on schizophrenia.

"All we have that would be accessible is the DSM—Diagnostic and Statistical Manual of Mental Disorders," the librarian replied.

"Show me where to look in it, if you could."

"Yes, I'll help you," she said cheerfully.

The librarian showed me to a comfortable chair, consulted the table of contents, and opened the thick book to where I should start reading.

It was laid out simply. A list of symptoms. A discussion of them. Likely outcomes. I read urgently, slightly embarrassed by my own curiosity.

It all fit, every bit of it.

The whole thing said nothing about mothers. I opened my purse and took the prescription slip out of my wallet. I remembered that horrible doctor in the Department of Psychiatry—his clipped silver mustache, his power over me. I looked for "SCHIZOPHRENOGENIC MOTHER" in the manual's various indexes. It wasn't there, or anywhere.

I didn't know what that meant, and I was confused. But they, all of them—those psychiatric types, Leah, probably Len and Jane too, and probably by now the Thatchers—held power over me, and they accused me. I could not budge them from myself any more than I could have budged a manhole cover on a street with a stick.

I thanked the librarian and gave her the book back.

Len had come home when I got back. He was sitting in his chair in the living room. It was only the middle of the day. I pulled the rocker up close to him so we could talk softly.

He looked out the picture window to the oak's turning leaves and said, "Johnny Scannell called me into his office at about ten. 'Len, you need some time off. Do you have any vacation time coming? You need to lighten up, get away on the weekends, get yourself a hobby or two. Have you thought of taking up golf? This isn't a warning', he said, 'just a friendly conversation. But if you find yourself at any time wanting to go back to the union, you could always transfer to Chicago or San Francisco.'"

Len pursed his lips as though he was trying to keep from crying. "If it just wasn't for that goddamn girl, I could make it. These have been the hardest four months of my life."

"She's killing you," I said.

"Yes, she's killing me."

Silence.

"I stopped by my doctor on the way home," Len continued. "He said there's nothing we can make her do, like see a psychiatrist, since she's of age now. He gave me some tranquilizers." He took a bottle of small, white pills out of his suit jacket. "Now I can just take some and go around like a zombie."

"All right, Len," I said. "All right."

I went to Leah's room, opened the door, and walked in. She raised her head from the bed, her dark hair all tousled around her face. I pulled the curtains open and let the September sun in. She squinted at me and reached to the floor for the box of Cheerios.

"I'm hungry," she said.

"Your father and I want to talk to you. I want you to put on your housecoat and come out to the living room."

"Huh?" She cocked her head. "I'm still sleepy. I want to sleep some more."

I cringed at her selfishness, selfishness without end. I ended up shouting. "GET UP NOW."

I walked out. I was clenching my hands, tears of exasperation in my eyes. I did not want to let her make this hard; Leah had a way of controlling by pushing me away. As I realized that, I kind of hated her.

"Hey, isn't there any fresh coffee?" Leah yelled a minute later from the kitchen.

She walked into the living room with a Coke. She hadn't bothered to put on her housecoat. She stood there in a see-through, shorty nightgown and bare feet. Embarrassed for Len, I went to get Leah's housecoat but couldn't find it in the messiness of her room. I put my jacket over her, and she made a little face.

She squinted some more at the early afternoon light from the backyard. "What's the big deal? That scene I made at the Thatchers' pretentious party?" She bowed her head and grimaced at her father.

Len stood up from his blue chair. "Don't you talk to me like that!"

"I'll talk to you any way I please."

Rage in his eyes, Len moved toward her.

"Len, don't!" I shouted.

He picked up the poker beside the fireplace, waving it hard around in the air. Then he took a deep breath, dropped the poker on the carpet, put his face in his hands, and started sobbing.

"Len, sit down," I pleaded. "Please, Len, just sit down."

He sat for a long minute, breathing hard, getting control of himself: first his hands, then his shoulders, then his face.

"Are you all right, Len?" I asked. He nodded feebly. I turned to Leah. "Sit down on the sofa."

She sat without a word. Then she took a big swig of her Coke. It fizzed out of the bottle onto the arm of my blue-and-white sofa.

I knew it would leave a permanent stain. It was just one more insane thing happening. I went over to the coffee table and picked up my purse. I opened it and pulled out a large envelope. "Here is a certified check made out to you for five-thousand dollars. I suggest you go to a bank, open an account, and deposit it. Then you can get yourself an apartment, or whatever you want to do."

"You're kicking me out? Seriously?"

"We want you to leave."

She didn't even bother to stare at me as she took the envelope and went to her room and slammed the door behind her.

"Did you give her your money?" Len spoke slowly, clearly stunned.

"It's my money," I said. Just as he had said twenty years earlier, when he brought home that brand-new Lincoln Continental.

Now, it was Len's turn to object. "That money was made by these hands." He held them up to me as they shook. "Do you think I enjoyed spending my life in apartment building basements, fixing washing machines, night after night, while you were home watching TV with those two brats?"

I almost said, "Well, at least you didn't have to be around us."

But I didn't say anything.

"That girl is my ward," Len said. "She's nothing but a ward. Holding us hostage with her fancy 'nervous breakdown.'

She controls you, and you can't see it. Now she's even taken all your money."

Len got up and went to our bedroom. Almost immediately, he came back out. "I'm going for a drive, as soon as I get in my overalls. I don't know where I'll go, and I don't know when I'll be back, either."

I, too, wanted to go somewhere. But I had nowhere to go. I'd already been at the library, and I had no one to visit. But I had to go somewhere. Going to the ranch would make me feel the same as staying home would. So I did something that surprised me utterly as I watched myself do it; I got my purse, got in my car, and drove to the airport.

Inside the terminal, I watched airplanes come in, people with smiles on their faces climb down the plane's steps, cross the tarmac, and arrive to hugs and handshakes.

I'd once taken a flight, just the girls and me, to Ohio. I'd sat beside a young man with tan hair and blue eyes. He was gentle and sensitive; I could tell from his voice. We got to talking, and told each other our lives and our secrets, all the way to Ohio. I was still young, and I would have followed him anywhere.

When I got back home, Leah was gone.

An ache, big as my whole body.

24

I thought Leah would call us.

She didn't.

It became chilly at about five o'clock. Had she taken her jacket? And her coat, for the approaching night? I got tears in my eyes. I couldn't bear to go into her room to see what she'd taken and what she'd left behind.

I sat by the purple-and-black afghan, which Morgan had taken over. He was in a circle, sound asleep. He hadn't cared about her one way or the other.

At nightfall, I wondered where Leah was, and I shivered. Was she walking a street downtown? I could imagine her witlessly following somebody home. Nighttime was danger—danger and cold.

I cried silently.

Len, who'd returned home an hour after I had, came into the living room and said, "She'll be all right. She'd call if she wasn't all right."

I closed my eyes, exhaling deeply. Could I stand this through the night?

What a mistake.

Was she lying on a bench in City Park, thieves in the blackness around her, or lying on a bench at a bus stop?

Leah had no friends except Susan. I wanted to go next door to ask Susan if she'd heard from her. But not if it meant facing Alice and Charles.

Len came into the living room again and said I'd only make myself sick by worrying. "Come to bed," he said.

I lay in my bed and listened to distant police sirens, distant trains going somewhere far. I lay there and waited for the front door to open.

The next morning, I got up before Len. I made coffee, then sat down in the dinette with a mug. I was hollow.

Had Leah remembered to take her toothbrush? That made me cry. Six o'clock in the morning, and I was crying.

Her bottle of blue pills was still on the lazy Susan.

Len made morning noises in the bedroom and the bathroom, then came into the kitchen. He just looked at me.

"She'll be all right, you wait and see," he said.

After he left for work, I leaned my head forward and cringed. Was she having cereal or toast with some horrible street man she'd gone home with the night before? Maybe she'd had no choice.

I could have behaved so much better yesterday. Then I closed my eyes and thought, *How?*

I knew I had to open her door. Go into her empty room.

Before Jane had stormed out in August, she'd folded her blankets and rolled her sheets up in a neat pile. But Leah's bed was just as it had been when I'd gotten her up. A few Cheerios lay on the carpet, and two or three in the folds of the sheet she'd been sleeping on.

Her suitcase was still in her closet. But her big leather bag—big enough to carry her cosmetics, one dress, and a change of underwear—was gone. Her pantsuit and best dress were missing. She must have put one or the other on before she left. I could see her thinking, planning. As I imagined her deciding, walking from closet to dresser, filling that burgundy bag, she seemed real again, almost there in the room.

I went back into the kitchen. Morgan wanted his breakfast; he was wreathing my ankles and crying that deep-throated Siamese cry like a human baby's. What if he were to go missing, Leah's cat? I'd search the house. I'd search the basement, among all the boxes, down under Len's desk. I'd search the backyard, and the shrubs in the front. As I went about my day, I'd listen hopefully for that ugly yowl, a cat wanting to be let in. I'd go outside and call for him, ask Alice and Susan to keep an eye out for him, maybe check with the neighbors across the alley. At some point, I'd walk up and down that alley—the path of the wide, heavy, screeching garbage trucks. Eventually, I'd get in my car and drive around the neighborhood, glancing in the gutters of the streets, fearing the worst. In two or three days, I'd somehow know for a fact that he'd been killed by a car or a dog, all while lost, confused, frightened—even hungry and thirsty.

I abruptly went back into Leah's room, leaving the cat hungry. I opened her jewelry box. Her key to the cabin at the ranch was gone.

Or maybe she'd kept it somewhere else. I looked through, under, inside everywhere.

How would she get to the ranch anyway? A girl alone, hitchhiking into the mountains, into the woods. It would be hard for her to do something more dangerous. No—anything she'd be doing right now would be dangerous.

I called the ranch and let the phone ring and ring.

Of course, I would need to give her time to get there.

That afternoon, I called the police. They had no information to give me. I called all the hospitals. Finally, I called Ft. Logan, the public mental hospital. But Ft. Logan didn't give out names.

I couldn't find my daughter.

When Len came home, he had Johnny Scannell all over his face: a man he had no control over, as I now had no control over Leah. Len stopped in front of me, standing in the middle of the kitchen. His face softened.

"I'm more worried about you than I am about Leah." Len was speaking low. When had he ever done that before? He reached in his pants pocket and got his little bottle of white pills. "Here, take one of these."

I took his tranquilizer. How funny, in a way.

It had no effect on me. I knew it wouldn't.

We sat in the dinette. Len didn't talk, and I didn't talk. Then I told him about the ranch key, the police, and the hospitals.

I got up to get something for dinner. I opened the refrigerator and suddenly felt heavy, thick headed. I went to lie down.

When I woke up, I knew it was far into the evening, because the bedroom was dark. Len was sitting in the living room, Morgan there again. Len was doing nothing.

"I fed the cat," he said. "Go get yourself something to eat. Then we're going to talk."

What Len said was that I should go up to the ranch the next day to see if Leah was there. If she was, I should bring her home. If she wasn't there, though, I should take a good walk in the woods, maybe over to the aspen grove across the meadow, maybe up the county road. I should just come to grips with things, relax, and calm down.

That's all he had to say.

I drove down Hampden until it became Highway 285 and I was out of the city. Almost immediately 285 turned into just two lanes and started curving slowly upward through Turkey Creek Canyon. There, through all the weekends of all the years I'd driven up to the ranch, my mind always wandered to shopping lists, bitter words spoken by my husband, the needs of our many animals. And the girls. Not long ago, that lovely conversation with Alice. Today my mind wandered to someone else's memory.

Somewhere around the turn of the last century, the old man from the other side of our mountain, who had helped Len fell and burn the beetle trees, had come across the prairie from Kansas, hundreds of hard miles, with a wagon full of all his possessions. He'd likely have stopped in little Denver, with its trading posts, to equip himself for his trip into the Rocky Mountains. He would then have driven his wagon—probably in the company of other homesteaders and the wife he'd found in Denver—on a trail through Turkey Creek Canyon's walls, ten-miles long: a journey in itself.

The canyon was perhaps a fifth of the way from Denver to the piece of homesteader land he would eventually claim. It wouldn't do his journey justice to name the hills, mountains, meadows, creeks, and gulches he passed after Turkey Creek Canyon. It wouldn't do it justice because likely those places didn't even have names then. Were there maps of the pioneer trails? Could he read a map?

I passed the Sky Village Inn to the left, passed mountain valleys with sweet grass that had turned into hay, the valleys now dotted with horses and a few cattle. At Field's Trading Post, I turned left, up the low mountain to Conifer. Then at Conifer Junction's fork, where there was a little white grange which doubled as a one-room schoolhouse, where a right turn went into heavy woods, I turned left into my ranch. Up at the cabin, the air was still, and it was remarkably cold for the end of September. I wanted so badly to find Leah there. She filled up my whole being. I wanted her to be like a cat come home, finally. I wanted happiness.

The door was still locked. Inside, the cabin was dusty and smelled of mice droppings and closed-up air.

I just stood there. This was the full depth of remorse.

To break the silence, I called Len at his office. Evelyn answered, transferred the call.

He was irritated to hear from me. "I've got a meeting in five minutes. What's wrong, anyway?"

I was surprised, after his kindness the night before. "I'm up at the ranch, and Leah isn't here."

"Well, dammit, solve that problem yourself. I'm busy now, so don't call back. Goodbye."

I felt like he had kicked me.

All the years of all of us here, coming and going here. Growing. Growing up. Growing rich. Growing bitter with each other. So bitter we would wince, turn our faces, walk away.

My remorse was savage. I wanted to tear a hole in myself.

And they told me *I* had caused all that. Strangers hundreds of miles away had told me that. Another stranger had even given me a technical name for the kind of person I was. I destroyed people, even my own child.

How everyone would be better off without me, especially Len. And Jane. Even Leah.

I had no desire to die, only to be rid of myself.

I pulled my old wooden chair over to the cupboard and climbed up on the seat. The gun was on top of the cupboard, and there was a small, dusty box of bullets. For some reason I wiped the gun off on my shirt so it would be shiny. I loaded it, got my brown leather jacket from the coat rack, and headed out.

It was already cold, deep fall in my woods, and maybe three o'clock. A crow cawed against the creamy sky. A few flakes of snow were falling. I tramped over brittle brown needles that had once been parts of green ponderosa clumps far above. I aimed to go as far as the old fence at the back of my dear woods, sit down, and shoot myself. Right in my ugly face.

I got almost to the rows of barbed wire and found a good tree. I put my back against it and slid down. I suddenly realized that pungent ponderosa sap was sticking to the back and the sleeves of the leather jacket. I mindlessly stood up and took off the jacket. Globs of yellow and little pieces of bark and wood dust stained it. And now I'd gotten them on my hands.

The sap summed up all my futility.

Leaning my forehead against the tree, I put my arms around its trunk and shivered and cried. I was too cold to kill myself.

I put the jacket back on, still warm from my body heat. The body heat changed everything. I sat back down on the ground, huddled in my jacket, and thought carefully, breathing in and out. Time went by. I crossed back and forth in my mind, thought everything through for yet another time. What I owed, what I was owed.

I took the hard black handgun and aimed it with both hands. And then I fired it, out into the woods.

I shook afterward, the sound of the gun ugly, shocking, obscene.

25

On the way back, I found my woods no longer enchanted me. They would not remain witness to me in any way, except for some dry needles broken by my footsteps, smeared globs of sap on a tree's bark, a little bullet—perhaps stuck in a trunk, perhaps on the ground—never to be found. The woods would exist for themselves, and for themselves alone. My little log house would retreat into the soil, or be broken up by someone for firewood or some such thing.

A little wind was picking up, and I was glad to get inside. I put the gun and the box of bullets back on top of the cupboard, pulling the chair back to where it belonged. I made a fire in the Ben Franklin stove and then, waiting for the cabin to get warm, put a frozen chicken pot pie in the oven.

From inside the bottom of the cupboard, I took an old bottle of sherry I'd bought in the days of Virginia Gunderson. I'd almost forgotten it was there. It was dusty, having long since been pushed to the back, behind canned goods and tin boxes.

It was getting warm in the kitchen. It struck me that I seldom sat over in the living room. But the big oak table was mine, the hub of my yellow kitchen. I had long ago asked Len to paint the walls yellow, because that was my favorite color. And now I sat at my table, on the chair I'd used to get to the gun, and sipped sherry from a ceramic mug.

Years of husband and girls going in and out of my kitchen, carrying implements of every kind—brushes, halters, butterfly nets, knives. The kitchen itself was a hub. And I was, and always had been, the hub of the hub. I had been in charge of everything and everyone in these four lives, without existing any more than my own mother had.

I had tried to exist. I could not. At one time I had been sure Virginia would help me exist, but she would not. Len, Jane, and Leah—I had been unnoticed by all. It was kind of all right that the girls hadn't noticed me. But it was not all right that Len hadn't.

Yet, I was not worth nothing. A slow, kind thought, that one, and it made me tingle with a sort of joy.

I had not done a bad job. No, I had not done a bad job.

The phone rang. Of course it was Len. Not Leah.

"Why are you still there?" he asked.

Before I could reply, he said, "Leah is at Denver General."

"In the psychiatric ward?"

"Yes. A Dr. Summers wants to see you at two o'clock tomorrow. You can see Leah after that."

"I'll be there."

"Well, it's too bad you had to hear it over the phone like this." Kindness.

"It's where she's supposed to be. She's safe."

"How late are you going to be tonight?"

"I'm spending the night up here."

"If you're sure …"

It occurred to me, after we hung up, that I'd never spent the night in the cabin alone. Not once in all those years. Actually, I'd seldom spent a night alone anywhere.

My chicken pot pie was ready; it smelled delicious.

I thought about that girl of mine as I broke the pie open and watched its steam rise. Leah took on the world headlong, with her beloved words of every kind. A smart-aleck. Eyes seeing far away—too far away. To somewhere I could never know.

I thought, *But I will accept Leah the way she is.*

Perhaps now I accepted myself for the way I was. Perhaps I did.

A cold night. I took blankets from Jane and Leah's beds.

I lay there. There were no lights anywhere at all. Coyotes howled from far down in the meadow.

Denver General Hospital was not somewhere I'd thought I would ever go. It was in a poorer section of the city, not far from the bad part of downtown. I wouldn't go in that neighborhood at night, driving alone. But people did in fact go there at all times. Nighttime gunshot wounds. Daytime falls off scaffolding. Car accidents. Overdoses. Heart attacks. Rape victims. Crazy people.

I turned off Spear Boulevard, yielded to an ambulance heading out—all flashing lights and siren shrieking—and entered the parking structure. A heavy middle-aged woman was pushing a young man in a wheelchair up the ramp. He was likely her adult child. I was filled with pity for another mother.

I stopped for her, but the car behind me let out a long blare. The woman, apparently thinking I'd done that, swung around at me in anger. I couldn't hear her shout because the man behind me beeped again, even longer.

The corridors of the first floor of Denver General were wide, gleaming with just-washed, pale-green linoleum and dotted with little orange "Caution" signs.

A sign by one of the elevators said "Psychiatric Unit Fourth Floor." I got in and was crowded to the side. I was the only person who got off at the fourth floor.

The wide glass doors of the unit were locked. A policeman stood just inside.

I was … what was I? I was not the Anne Hope who had, months before, gone at dawn halfway across the country to find her terrified daughter, comfort her, somehow rescue her from an unknown enemy. This time I was not even weary. In youthful slang, I was a pro.

The nondescript woman at the glass-paneled reception station told me to take a seat in the central waiting area. At the far end of the area, I noticed a glass door with a sign that read "AA meeting in progress."

After ten minutes or so, the meeting was apparently over, and men, who seemed somehow bent into themselves, came out of that room. Then the receptionist was coming over to me, pointing out the woman beside her—gray haired, tapping toward me with the white-and-red pole of the blind. That woman held her hand out toward me and introduced herself as Dr. Summers.

"I understand Leah is your daughter. She's a lovely young woman, Mrs. Hope." Dr. Summers smiled in my direction. "Let's go to my office."

There, she turned on the overhead light, the standing lamp beside each of the visitor's chairs, and, sitting down, a big light on her desk. She came to life in a new way, seemingly sure of herself. She leaned her pole in a corner.

Focused on me, Dr. Summers smiled again. "I'm so glad Leah has someone. She wouldn't talk when she was first brought here, and she just had a California driver's license, so we didn't know."

I leaned forward. "How is my daughter?"

"She's doing better today, Mrs. Hope. She was found by the police in an alley, delusional, three nights ago. What do you know about her illness?"

"I have some reason to think she has schizophrenia." I told this woman about California, about Leah's hospital stay there, the blue pills she didn't take, her behavior in Denver, how we'd asked her to leave, the money I'd given her.

"Can you imagine, Dr. Summers, what it's like to ask your own daughter to leave your home …" My voice caught.

She leaned forward so that we were looking steadily into each other's eyes.

"I don't believe that I can imagine that," Dr. Summers said slowly. "But I can imagine you've felt that you've lost your daughter in several ways since this began happening."

"What can be done for Leah at this point?"

"We've put her on an antipsychotic medication we've had good results with. She came in here very somber. We know she wasn't molested, but her night in the street seems to have had a profound impact on her. She told me this morning that she now realizes how sick she can get, and she doesn't want to go back to being that way again. Personally, I don't think she's going to have to. By the way, do you want me to write down for you the name of the medication we have her on?"

"Yes, I ..." My voice caught again. "Schizophrenia is treated with medication, isn't that right?"

"Yes, that's right."

"Well, if it's a medical condition, then why do they say that bad mothers cause it?"

Dr. Summers frowned to herself in a way that made me think she'd been asked that question before. By another mother? How many mothers?

"I've been a psychiatrist for over thirty years," said Dr. Summers. "I've seen every sort of mother to schizophrenics—bad mothers, good mothers, indifferent mothers (if there can be such a thing), mothers who've been beaten down flat by their own suffering over this. You don't need to become one of the latter, Mrs. Hope."

In the room's bright lights, her clear, intelligent eyes shined. "I think Leah's going to be all right. She'll get much better. Not well, but better. Whether she'll eventually be able to live on her own and to work, I don't know. She's got good prognosis factors. And she's got spunk. We'll keep her here for perhaps a week, and then I'll see you again, and one of our social workers will help you find a place for her to live."

A place for my daughter to live. That struck me hard. I felt tears starting to well, but I blinked hard and took a deep breath. "You've been very kind, Dr. Summers."

"Please pardon me if I don't walk you out, Mrs. Hope. A nurse can come show you to Leah. She is looking forward to seeing you." Dr. Summers reached for her phone.

My daughter was silent as she came down the closed hall to meet me. She was wearing her own green trousers, but a dark-blue hospital top. Her hair was combed. She laid her forehead on my shoulder and hugged me hard. Silently. She wouldn't let go. The young nurse who was with her separated us, then took Leah and me to a little sitting room with three vinyl-covered chairs. She showed Leah which chair to sit in.

"We have coffee at the nurses' station. Would you like some?" the nurse asked. When I smiled and shook my head, she smiled back and left.

"Thank you for coming, Mother." Leah was looking down at the floor. What was Dr. Summers' word? Somber.

"Are they attacking you with razors again, Leah?" I whispered.

"The medicine they're giving me makes that stuff go away."

"What else?"

"Lots of things are going away."

"Why were you in that alley so late at night?"

"The Evil Beings told me I had to do that so I would be killed by someone with a knife."

"Why did you have to be killed?"

"Because I'm bad."

"Are you really bad, Leah?"

She was silent.

"Are you really bad?"

Leah looked up at me, slowly. "The Evil Beings told me that if I revealed that I'm not bad, they'd kill me. But I'm telling you now. No, Mother, I'm not really bad."

"See, you said it, and they didn't kill you."

She got a big smile on her face. "Astounding."

"Is anyone really bad?" I asked.

"No, no one's really bad." Then she hesitated, looking me full in the face. She drew her breath in sharply.

Oh, no. I felt the attack coming.

"Well, maybe that guy who trotted up to me that night—right up to my face—out of some corner of the alley and said, 'Gimme your purse.' I scratched his face all the way down with my fingernails. He looked amazed. Then he trotted away, wiping his face with his hand. But he didn't get my purse."

My daughter, who'd been in such danger that night, was inured by it enough to tell me her story in a nonchalant voice.

"When I got here—a couple of policemen brought me—the nurse took my purse and my earrings and the change in my pockets. I guess they give them back when you get out." Leah cocked her head. "When do I get out?"

"When you're better."

"Where will I go?"

"They'll help us find some place. Dr. Summers said they would."

"She's the lady who can hardly see, isn't she? But she's cool."

"Yes. She is."

Two evenings later, Len put aside his own troubles and went down after dinner to see Leah. He left with a frown on his face, whether about her or about having to drive in that neighborhood, I couldn't tell. He wasn't gone long.

Back in the dinette, he still had the frown.

"How is she today?" I asked.

"She looked fine to me. But I can't tell the difference. She said she'd be discharged next week. I hope you know what you're doing."

He seemed to want to say something else, but couldn't quite. "That's some setup they've got down there."

"If we were still working for BF Goodrich, that's where we'd go," I observed.

"Well, we're not still working for BF Goodrich. Imagine my daughter being there." He looked out the side window to the dark street, angry.

"Knock it off, mister, that is where she is."

Then Len got around to what he wanted to say. "I got your check back from Leah. She told the nurse I could have it, and the nurse got it from Leah's possessions."

"That's Leah's money," I said. "To take care of her when she's discharged."

"Well, I don't want her handling it. She'd just spend it, like buying that big ugly purse. Put the check in your jewelry box for now."

I realized his anger was now turning to me.

"You know, that five-thousand dollars, someday you'd have had a lot of money from it, if you hadn't just handed it over to that girl. But of course, you still own our ranch, all by yourself."

Len sounded as if a woman and a girl had stolen big from him, and there was nothing he could do about it.

Leah liked Dr. Summers, and the doctor liked her too, I gathered. She knew about Leah's languages, travels, education. Dr. Summers announced she knew of the "perfect" psychiatrist. He was in Boulder: an hour away.

I took Leah to see Dr. Warner. He was British, about fifty, and it turned out that he and his wife had a summer house in Italy. Dr. Warner and Leah spoke Italian together, and she fell in love with him—just like that. He had curly brown hair and a short curly beard. A warm teddy bear, Leah told me later. Dr. Warner spoke with her in private for half an hour, and then he asked her to sit outside while he talked with me, with her permission. He told me right away that his specialty was schizophrenia and he believed in recovery.

"Mrs. Hope, I'd love to work with Leah, and I'm very, very happy to have met her mother." Dr. Warner gave me an impish smile. Then he said seriously, "Please do call me anytime you have the need."

He called Leah back in. "I'd like you to spend some time—a month, two months, or as long as you need—in a halfway house here in Boulder that I work with. It's called 'Lost and Found.' You won't be able to have your own room, but it's warm and cheery, and I imagine you'll like all the young people who are living there now."

Leah and I went back to Crestmoor Park to get some clothes and favorite book for her new room in Boulder.

"The piano's gone," Leah said.

"Yes, your father had them come get it on Monday. You can take it up again someday, you know."

"I will take it up again someday. You wait and see." She got out her suitcase and started filling it. "Do you want me to leave my room bare?"

"Don't talk that way, Leah. When you want, later on, perhaps you can come down to Denver for a weekend now and then."

"Yeah, that would be cool."

"Yes, it would."

It wasn't that Alice and I didn't become friends again. From our backyards, we waved, said "Hi." We remarked on the now-bare trees, the joy of her dogs running through the yard, the impending winter. A week after Leah had moved to Lost and Found, I had Alice over for coffee and told her all that had happened.

Alice thanked me for filling her in, and she took my hands in both of hers, and said, "Thank you, Anne, thank you for telling me. That was bravery."

But I had, just by being Leah's mother, spilled blood on the floor of my friendship with Alice. And I could tell that it wasn't because of the mess of my daughter's tantrum at the Thatchers' party. It was the fact that Leah had endangered Susan's hard-sought and hard-won sanity at the Denver Dry Tea Room. A mother doesn't put up with that sort of thing, not even from the daughter of her own best friend.

Thus, I had sort-of lost Alice, so dear to me.

Sort-of lost. So maybe I hadn't totally.

I started to hope again, about an outside chance of things being back the way they were supposed to be. Sure, no one wants to get their hopes up too high. But I could get my hopes up just right, so I could bear it if I lost. I wouldn't dwell on Leah or Alice returning to me just as they had been before. Instead, I'd examine my hopes like shiny Christmas bulbs, a bit each day, then put them away for a while. I wouldn't dwell. But I wouldn't fear, either. Between Mrs. Hunter in California and the black gun in the woods, I'd had enough of both hopelessness and fear.

26

Len was lying on his bed when I got back at 2:30. He'd come home early, overwhelmed by stomach pain. He pointed to where it was crushing him. "If I have to throw up, it's going to kill me." He breathed heavy breaths, groaned, grimaced.

I sat helpless on my bed beside his, watching his labor. "Len," I said, "let me call your doctor."

"I do not need any doctor."

"Yes, you do."

He moaned, turning his face from me to the wall.

Half an hour later, he whispered to me to call his doctor. The doctor relayed orders: one of the tranquilizers, chicken broth, no dinner, perhaps some Jell-O later. Tomorrow Len was to take the day off and come in for a complete physical. And he was to consider going on a vacation soon.

After savoring its odor, Len sipped the chicken broth. His face and shoulders relaxed as the broth reached his stomach and momentarily covered the pain over with its slippery heat. But the pain came back within minutes. He took to walking slowly through the house, his fist on his stomach. The rest of the afternoon passed slowly, and the evening was a slow ordeal too.

Once Len was in bed, he found sleep out of the question. He lay like an embryo, surrounding his pain with his body. He was tired, and his breathing became a bit raspy, which frightened me. He moaned. But then, about two o'clock in the morning, he fell asleep.

So I was able to sleep too.

The nurse called early. Len could have a ten o'clock appointment, but he was to consume nothing but black coffee or tea beforehand. Haggard from his night, he sat down at the dinette to a mug of tea. The weak October sun shone over the table.

"Do you suppose they'll find something really wrong, like my mother's cancer?" Len asked.

I found myself feeling for the man. "No, Len, it won't be that."

I spent the slow, slow morning doing nothing. I couldn't stop thinking about how scared he was.

At about noon, Len walked in. He sat down at the dinette table and slapped his hand down on it, like he had when he got the supervisor's job. "The doctor said it isn't cancer. But I have such high blood pressure that it's going to kill me unless I make some changes."

He looked exhausted by the news. I didn't know what to say to comfort him. I was surprised at how much I wanted to ask him if he was scared, but I could never do *that*. Yet at least it wasn't cancer. At least not that.

"Would you like me to fix you some breakfast?" I asked.

"Goddamn it, didn't you hear a word I said?"

"Yes, I did, Len. Do you want some breakfast?"

He nodded, overwhelmed by everything, including me. I was right, too. He needed food and sleep.

Len rose in the early afternoon. I fixed him some lunch. He was deep in thought while he ate. Then he pushed his chair back. He put on his oration tone. "I'm working on killing myself, the doctor said. It's only a matter of time. Something's got to give."

"Well, at least Leah's part in it is getting taken care of."

"And not any too soon. That leaves Johnny Scannell. Either he goes or I go. It's that simple. I did some thinking while I was lying in bed just now, after I woke up. The solitude did me good."

"And what conclusion did you come to?"

"I'm willing to go back to being a regular dispatcher. That means giving up the supervisor job. I'm willing to do that to get that S.O.B. off my back. But we'd have to move to San Francisco, so I could work in the dispatchers' office there, out of his control. That would mean selling the Mile-High Washing Machine Rental and selling this house."

He sat back and waited for me to object.

I said I would not leave before Leah was properly settled in. And I didn't want to leave this house. I didn't want to leave Denver.

"But if you did decide to go to San Francisco anyway," I added, "I could follow you there, maybe next year. You'd have to live there alone for a while."

He wiped his mouth again with his napkin. "We could live on Nob Hill and go to the ocean and eat at Fisherman's Wharf and drive to see the wine country on the weekends."

"I'd do that next year, but not now."

"You know goddamn well I couldn't live like that. Once again that girl's more important to you than anything else."

I felt sorry for Len because he wasn't able to say, *I couldn't do that without you.* I felt sorry that I couldn't say, *Of course, I know it would be hard for you, a middle-aged man alone in a big city.* And he was, after all, a man who'd never been alone, who'd gone straight from his parents' home to marry. Right now he was against a wall, no way through it, no way around it, no place to turn. This was a completely defeated man who had to get up tomorrow morning and go to the office and submit himself to his superior, whom he hated.

Pity was new in my heart, wasn't it? I'd first felt it when I turned the gun barrel away, into the trees. That was pity for myself. Now I felt it for Len. It spread slowly through my body, and made me want to meet his eyes with mine.

27

"How's Father?" Leah asked when I arrived in the middle of the morning.

That was the first thing she asked me, peering beyond her self-absorption. Did she actually care?

"He has too many burdens to bear," I replied. "I don't know how else to put it. I'm very worried about him, and so is Jane. She calls him every evening now."

Leah looked sad. The sadness didn't really take over her thickly medicated face, but I could see it there, especially in the lines on her forehead.

We were alone in the Victorian parlor of Lost and Found, full of second-hand furniture. I stood back and looked my daughter over. She was letting her hair grow—the lower half was dull and Clairol brown-black, and the new half was her own shiny black hair. She'd managed to cut herself some bangs, which were entirely black, of course. The mixed result perfectly framed the face that was half there, half in some other world.

All in all though, these were vast improvements. I told her so.

"I'm going to be perfect by the time I'm thirty," she replied.

"You have a long way to go."

"Yes, I know. I'm only twenty-three."

"That's not what I mean."

"You're funny, Mother."

Leah went to the kitchen to get us coffees, while I waited on the green sofa, its cloth darkened by overuse. Which was good, I thought; perhaps there were a lot of visitors, so the kids who lived here weren't just staying upstairs.

Leah returned. "I want to show you my room."

I followed her up the stairs, two flights. I wondered why they used to make houses so big. Oh, I knew—all the grandparents and aunts and uncles and so forth. The carpet, old and also green, here threadbare, there frayed, made the stairwell dark. Leah's own room had a high ceiling and one window. Three metal beds in a row filled it. A radiator made the room too hot, but Leah didn't seem to notice. So, this was a halfway house.

"Let's sit on my bed."

I took a sip of coffee and put my mug on the floor beside me.

"Have you looked closely at the tiny flowers in the wallpaper?" I asked her.

"Oh, I love the wallpaper. This room is incredibly cozy. Especially at night. The night lights from the Pearl Street Mall make shimmers on the ceiling."

"Where are your roommates right now?"

"Oh, that's a sad story. I mean, Jenny's story isn't sad. She's a heroin addict who's kicking it. She has huge pink scars on her wrists, so it must have been really awful. But she's very cheerful. I think she's at a Narcotics Anonymous meeting right now. Or AA. She practically lives at meetings, except when she's here sleeping. She's nice, really, she is. I know she's going to make it. I just know it."

"What's the sad story, Leah?"

"That was Tracy. She was cute, and roly-poly. But she was manic-depressive. Last week she kept getting more and more manic. She was wiggling around on top of her bed, and talking to me a mile a minute about everything that popped into her head, and you should have seen her eyes; they were on fire. Over the weekend, she went bonkers, jumping up and down, and you couldn't understand her anymore. They came and gave her a shot and took her away. I don't know what's going to happen to her. I don't know how I could find out, either. I hope she'll be okay, but I don't think she will. Can you imagine being that way? It's awful, just awful."

"I'm so sorry, Leah. Do you have someone to talk to about these girls?"

"Oh yeah, I talk to Dr. Warner all the time. He said making friends is part of my getting well."

"How is the getting well coming?"

"You're uncomfortable sitting like that, aren't you? You're all hunched over like an old lady. There's a chair out in the hall. Let me get it for you."

"That's kind."

Leah returned with the chair, and then continued. "'How's the getting well coming?' Well, part of it is up to me, and part of it isn't. What I need is a roadmap. Isn't that funny?"

"No, Leah—I can see what you're saying."

"The hallucinations—the Evil Beings and all that stuff—they're gone. Because of the pills Dr. Warner is giving me. 'Better Living through Chemistry,' right? Paranoia is the hardest part now. I'm always wanting to call Father up in the middle of the night and ask him, again and again, if he hates me. I don't understand why it makes him so mad when I ask him. Sometimes I'm afraid all of you hate me, even Dr. Warner. Whenever it wants to, the paranoia rolls through me, and it follows its own rules."

I finished my coffee. "I don't think anybody hates you."

Then it was time for Leah to go fix sandwiches for everybody's lunch. Another resident would put out fruit; someone else would make a new pot of coffee.

For now, I left my daughter in Lost and Found, watched over and guided by Dr. Warner. But Leah had a little door open in her eyes, and there was a sign on it that read "The Future."

When I was driving home on the turnpike, the vast Eastern Plains were to my left and beyond. I knew them only as flatness: home to antelope, rabbits, coyotes, snakes. Winter would be coming upon them, and staying alive would be hard.

I was glad Leah's room was warm. And that she liked it. A new girl would be coming, a girl with a new story to draw Leah even further out of her self-preoccupation.

But did she still blame me? She never said anything about that these days. I really did know I didn't cause her illness, but in the illogic of love, I still felt so guilty.

I drove back toward Len, who now needed me more than Leah did.

28

Since it was early evening in the middle of October, orange light still glowed from behind the mountains to the west, making the tops of the peaks look like how embers used to, in our fire pit at the ranch. Up there, Len and I and the girls would huddle, sometimes with jackets and blankets, in chairs around that orange, and above us were the stars. At the end, when there was no fire anymore, the sky around us would get so dark we could see the long cloudy arc of the Milky Way spread over its top.

Of course, here, from a city backyard surrounded by houses with lights, no stars were to be seen. Which was just as well, really.

Len and I sat outdoors by the picture window. He in his wicker chair, I in Jane's. Jane who wasn't planning on coming back.

What about her father? Wouldn't she come back even for her father? I wondered.

The end of Len's cigar glowed. "Today I sent the weather report to the pilot. Johnny Scannell walked in and saw that I had just done that without his double-checking it. He slapped the papers he was carrying onto a desk and came right up to my face. We yelled at each other. In front of all the rest of the office. All the boys looked up at us. Nobody made a sound. God, was I angry. So I walked over to the emergency phone and called the tower. They ordered the pilot to turn around and taxi back. Nobody made a sound, not even Johnny."

Len looked out into the backyard. Dusk was gone. "At that moment I realized my career was over."

He drew from his cigar, then tilted his head back and exhaled oh-so slowly.

"Len," I said, "it's all going to be all right. You'll manage somehow. You'll be all right."

Len wanted to ask me what to do. The words hovered at his lips. Instead he said, "It would be nice if I just knew what to do."

We sat in silence until he was tired of his cigar.

"How about I make us some sandwiches?" I asked. "I can bring them out."

"You do that."

In a few minutes, I brought two jackets out and pulled the little table at the edge of the patio over between us, and we ate our ham sandwiches while wrapped in thought.

Eventually I said, "It's getting cold. I'm going to go inside in a minute."

"Fine. I'm just going to stay out here awhile."

"Len, do you remember when we first got married, and you said you were going to be a millionaire by the age of thirty?"

"By the age of thirty. Yeah."

"You can have the time now. All the time you want. You can grow the Mile-High Washing Machine Rental. You can make it big. Len, now you can become a millionaire."

"You won't move to San Francisco?"

"No, I won't. I won't see my husband demoted."

I went in with the plates and glasses and left him with his thoughts out there. I hadn't told him that I felt proud of him; a man who'd once worked in the rubber pits at BF Goodrich in Akron, who had then spent twenty years as a weatherman for United Airlines in Denver. A man who had never complained of being tired from working the midnight shift. Who'd never until today made a mistake, who'd never harmed anyone or anything at United in all that time, who'd been given the big responsibility as a dispatcher of aircraft. A man who'd made a very decent salary for his professional white-collar work, who could hold his head up around the likes of Charles Thatcher. A man who'd come a long way: Leonard Hope.

Well, he surely must have known I was proud of him, even if I didn't say it.

When Len came back in, he went to his little office down in the basement. I heard him talking on the phone. He talked for quite a while. Then he came up to the kitchen, where I'd just finished tidying up and feeding the cat.

"Jane's coming to see me for the day on Saturday. I'm paying her way since she can't afford it herself. She'll spend the night at the airport Marriott and then fly back home on Sunday. That way you won't need to straighten up for her, or cook her dinner."

Or, I thought, *even see her.*

Len wore his suit when he went to the airport for Jane. He also took with him his heavy brown jacket. That meant they'd be going up to the ranch. Of course Jane would want to go up to the ranch. They'd make a fire in the Ben Franklin stove, and Jane would fix a pot of coffee, and they would sit at the big oak table, and father and daughter would talk about Minneapolis, library school, Alan's studies, their plans for the future, and the rest of Len's life. He would tell her what he would never tell me: his hopes and dreams, his fears. Then they'd discuss me at length. Or perhaps they wouldn't discuss me at all. Perhaps they wouldn't ruin their perfect day together.

Jane would take a big jacket from the coat rack, and they'd go to the cliffs to see the view, over the first mile of the road that went around the mountain to where the old man lived, then down to the meadow and the spring, and over to the aspen grove where the Queen Anne's Lace grew in the summer. By now, in the mountain cold of mid-October, the aspens had lost their yellow and orange leaves; they were just white-and-black branches and twigs. Len and Jane would walk lovingly through their beautiful land, and they would resent me out loud for owning it.

My life with Jane was over. She hadn't called me "Mother" since our first horrible talk when she'd gotten back from Africa. I wondered if she knew that I loved her. My firstborn.

No, she didn't even think that I cared for her at all, and never had. And she didn't want me anyway; she had stretched a barbed-wire fence between us.

My firstborn. I could not even glimpse the way Jane and Len clung to each other in the face of me. Was that what love was?

When Len came back home late Saturday night, he put his coat and suit jacket away and switched into bedclothes. We went to sit in the dinette, me in my nightgown. We must have looked old and cozy. Len only said that the ranch was dry and colorless. Winter would come in any day now.

"Do you remember the surprise blizzard at the end of October last year, that you and Charles got caught in?" I asked.

Len winced at the mention of Charles. Gone now, thanks to Leah.

I realized my mistake of bringing the memory up. "How is my daughter?" I asked, changing the subject.

"Jane is fine. She says hello."

Now *I* winced. There was a little bit of cruelty to "She says hello." After all, she might have at least called, said a few words. Len seemed oblivious to that part of Jane which I'd seen so many times. I suddenly thought of when she saw me with the dying moth, and all the other times when she saw me with Alan: all that superiority over me. I winced.

"We stopped at the Hi-Lander Inn when we got to the highway, and we had steak sandwiches there." Len paused, then added, "The four of us never went to the Hi-Lander Inn, did we?"

"Yes, Len. Virginia Gunderson took us there for dinner once. We all had steaks. Don't you remember that?"

"That old babe. Someday I'm going to be as rich as her."

"Len …"

"I've decided I'm going to do what you want me to do, grow the Mile-High Washing Machine Rental. You've had good advice twice now. The first time was when you insisted we get the ranch."

He looked me in the eye, frowned, and smiled a little smile. "Now I'm going to retire from United, like you said. I'm going to get rich."

29

Leah—weekly, almost daily improving—moved on, to a house of enchantment, thanks again to Dr. Warner. Today I was visiting for the first time, and Leah's landlady, Mrs. Marsh, was showing me around.

"Do you know what that is, Mrs. Hope?" We stood at the threshold of a room with a puzzle.

I went into the room and looked at it closely. A slab of stone and a big metal cylinder. I thought back to typewriting. Typewriters had round tubes that worked as presses, against the striking keys, with the paper in between them. And so did mimeograph machines. I saw the similarity, even though the machine here was thick and heavy.

"Yes, the press is the principle of it," said Mrs. Marsh. "This is a lithograph press. When Leah comes back, she can tell you the Greek that 'lithograph' comes from."

Then Mrs. Marsh took me to her art studio. It was in the attic of the red Victorian house Leah now called home. The studio was a complete mess—cans, maybe twenty variously squeezed tubes of paints, half-painted pictures discarded and thrown on the floor, finished pictures hung to dry on the walls, brushes, several palates, aprons. A feeling of work and expectancy.

"What a beautiful picture you're painting there," I said to Mrs. Marsh.

"I love to work in watercolor," the beautiful woman replied. "It's a Greek island. My husband and I saw it last summer. Leah has already picked out another watercolor I just painted yesterday. It's a Greek side street. She wants to hang it in her room. Let's go there; she won't mind. Anyway, I imagine she'll be back soon."

Leah's room was down on the second floor, beside a room whose open door revealed a white stone sculpture in progress, on a high table. No one was there. "Lynn's gone home for the afternoon," said the landlady. "Leah likes Lynn, she told me she likes the music Lynn plays on her tape recorder while she works. They're about the same age, like the same stuff in general."

Leah's room was small, cozy with its big, old-fashioned bed and chest of drawers.

I smiled at the chest. "You know, when Leah was a baby, we had no money to speak of, and Leah and her sister both slept in drawers like these."

Mrs. Marsh shook her thick waves of black-and-gray hair, which ended in tight curls. "My goodness, that would have been over twenty years ago. Imagine, her a tiny baby." She looked around the room, smiling to herself; Leah had covered most of the walls with oil paintings, watercolors, and lithographs which Mrs. Marsh said she'd been storing. My daughter had mixed them all together. They were mostly paintings of forests, which I thought was an odd choice for Leah. But they weren't dark like the woods at the ranch. They were open and full of robust trees with broad leaves, which let sun through to make big mottled patches of light on the ground.

"Please, call me Ruby," Mrs. Marsh said suddenly.

"Thank you. And I'm Anne."

I was worried by Leah's extravagance, already on display here. "I hope you don't mind my daughter's style, Ruby. She can be, well, unconventional. Pictures covering every inch ..."

"Leah has a place here. I knew that the moment I heard about her from Dick Warner. She's been here a week, and she's been a delight. I'm sure you know Dick's a friend of mine, has been for years. I'd asked him if he knew someone in Boulder who could teach me a little Italian—my husband and I are going to Florence and Rome next summer—and of course he thought of Leah, saying she needed a room anyway. It just fell into place."

"Is she all right living here? I mean, is she all right here for you?"

"Absolutely. We have an Italian lesson every day before I go home. My husband's going to join us on the weekends. Leah's a good teacher. She's going to keep the ground floor clean, and do dishes and the like. Lynn and I have lunch here every day. Leah will make us sandwiches and do the shopping. And it means someone will be here in the evenings, so the place will look lived in."

"I hope she'll make this worthwhile for you, Ruby."

"She already has. But here's some more good news. Another friend of mine, Pam, who owns Dolphin Travel on the Boulder Mall, is willing to take Leah on to do some general work—filing and typing—starting in January. If that works out, perhaps Leah could eventually work her way up to travel agent. Anyway, Pam knows Dick, too, because Dick goes to Italy several times a year. He has a house there."

"I wish I had some way of expressing how all this is making me feel," I said. My voice was shaky, I realized, and tearful. I felt more alive than I had in years. Newer.

"The pleasure is everyone's. Think about it—everyone's," the beautiful woman with the beautiful house said.

There, out the window from her room, I saw Leah coming down the street, a grocery bag in each arm. Then my daughter was home. Down in the kitchen, past the living room with its storage bin for paintings, Leah put the sacks on the counter and hugged Ruby and then me. In that order, which actually made me glad. She was proceeding on in her life, one way or another. Today she moved gracefully, and her expressions were back to normal. She was a girl again, not just a caricature of one. Dr. Warner was clearly an artist, in his own field of work.

And I saw how much Leah and Ruby resembled each other. Both were tall and thin and had unruly dark hair, and both were wearing bandanas to control it a bit. The two wore dangly earrings, old t-shirts, and blue jeans. And both had beautiful features and bright, enthusiastic faces. I was passing my daughter along.

We were content with so little then, both Leah and I. A rented room and menial labor, with typing and filing promised for the near future. I thought of that horrible job she had interviewed for before she left our house and went out into the night; they'd asked her to hold a stick to point out words on a board in a conference room. No, this was not *literally* better, but it was tremendously better for Leah. She'd entered a big red Victorian house of wholesome work, beautiful work, where she was appreciated for being her zany self.

30

Len always kept his eyes steady on the road when he drove. Sitting beside him, I looked at the prairie land to the left, halfway back from Boulder.

Len said, "Someday all that's going to be businesses and apartment buildings—I mean, complexes. Apartment complexes are what they're building now."

"They'll need washers and dryers."

"Won't they though."

I looked at Len's profile. I saw the right half of the big smile which meant he was entirely happy. It was not his public, puckered-up smile that meant he'd either impressed or been impressed. This big smile was just right for a man on the open road, his future ahead of him.

"Just think—you're retiring from United exactly one month from today," I said.

"I've got a lot to do before December 1st, if I'm going to land running."

Would he miss the big planes, the roar of it all, the bustle, the awesome responsibility? The weather maps—when he looked up and out at the sky, would he still, almost automatically, analyze and calculate them?

I had no idea what Len would mourn, anger over, chuckle at. What he would look forward to, unconsciously licking his upper lip. I didn't know if he was afraid.

Figuring out the details of the pension he would receive when he left seemed to be foremost in his mind. He stopped mentioning the boys in the office. He stopped mentioning Johnny Scannell.

"What do you think? Do you really like where Leah's living now?" I asked him.

"Yes. She seems happy. And it's a pretty good deal. Almost no rent—can you imagine that?"

"Well, she's going to start paying more when she gets her job at the travel agency."

"And she seems to have a good doctor." He changed the subject. "That was a nice painting you bought from Leah's landlady. She said she made it herself, didn't she? It's kind of odd, but it was just what you wanted, right?"

A chalk drawing of brown pine needles—their actual size—dropping down through the air. No ground below. Just pine needles drifting at all angles through the air. No sound. Time captured. Motion captured. The arcs of the needles like something out of the girls' mathematics books. Thin, but whole.

It was a large picture, so I had no idea where I'd put it. Some place Len wouldn't particularly notice. After all, he thought it was odd, even though I knew it wasn't.

"I was glad to buy it for you. You can have anything you want. I don't want to get to the end of your days and mine having to think, 'She could have had anything she wanted, but she didn't say a word to me.'"

Was Len realizing, somewhere deep inside himself, that he truly cared for me? I turned and stared at the open land, the miles of it, and felt good. Good enough.

"Everyone can draw," Ruby said.

"Everyone?" I asked. "Maybe Leah can draw. Jane can."

"I'll bet you can draw, too."

"Oh, no, I'm not artistic at all."

Ruby went to a large cabinet by the storage bin. When she opened it, I could see that it held her paper supplies. She brought back a square piece of beautiful, thick, off-white paper, about eighteen inches wide, and sat down right beside me.

We were at the round table by her kitchen. Leah was gone, to see Dr. Warner. I'd come up to Boulder to bring my daughter towels and blankets and odds and ends she'd asked for.

Ruby had at some point penciled a circle about twelve inches across in the center of the paper. She handed me a black pen. "It's not like a ballpoint pen, but it does have a rounded nib. You'll see how easily it slides over the paper."

I had no idea what to do. What a fool I was going to make of myself in front of Ruby.

Ruby noticed. "Everybody's that way until pen touches paper. Then it's magic and you're free to draw. All you have to do then is make loose patterns—circles, leaves, flowers, little faces—just inside the pencil line, around and around, until you've reached where you started. Make your patterns about an inch big, more or less. You'll be surprised. Anne, take your pen and go."

I put pen to paper.

"Let the pen move into a curve," Ruby continued to instruct. "Turn that into a little leaf. Make another curve. Turn that into a face."

I could do all that. I could.

"Let one line suggest another. Let the pen be in charge."

My pen gained speed. It had a life of its own. That sounded corny, but I said it to Ruby anyway.

"Yes, a life of its own. As a teacher of mine told me years ago, 'Take your hands off the steering wheel.'"

So I watched myself draw. I didn't exactly know what I'd drawn, but when Ruby said it was beautiful, I was awed.

When I'd finished the first band, Ruby told me to make a second one inside it.

I drew around and around until the whole pencil circle was full except for a two-inch hole in the middle. I paused, amazed at how lovely my drawing was. A feeling of pleasure that was, well, foreign to me. I tried to hide how proud I was of myself, but Ruby said, "Look at you, Anne, you're an artist."

I was awed. "Should I fill it in? I'd like to, but I like it this way, too."

"This is where you have to have an aesthetic eye," Ruby explained. "Do you see that the empty space gives the picture breathing room? It suggests a round-and-around movement to what you have drawn."

"Yes …"

"Don't worry. You would have come to that on your own. It's a matter of trusting your reactions to what you see."

I put my pen down. "Everything in life seems to be a matter of trusting your reactions, Ruby."

"Boy, don't we learn that the hard way."

"The hardest thing I've had to learn is to trust my feeling that Leah's going to be okay, even when I'm gone."

"Stay for lunch today. It's 11:30, and Leah will be back soon. She'll fix us some sandwiches. In the meantime, let's put your drawing back in the cabinet so it won't get mussed up, and I'll tell you a story about knowing your child is going to be all right."

When Ruby sat down again, her eyes scanned the ceiling as she thought back to something, "Our middle son was—and still is—David. All three of them were good boys. When each one got to be sixteen and driving, Bruce and I would hold a family discussion before they drove somewhere to be with their friends. We asked where they were going, how long they would stay, what other kids would be there, what they planned on drinking. No drinking and driving, none at all, was at the center of every talk.

"We had a foreign exchange student living with us that winter, Peter, from Germany. Our oldest son—David's older brother—was Peter's 'host brother.' We all loved Peter, who was funny and up for anything fun. We were looking forward to a happy Christmas, all of us together, a German-American Christmas.

"Anyway, it was the first Saturday evening of December, and David was going to drive our Jeep to a small party with some of his high school friends, at a parent's house. It all sounded fine. We knew many of the boys, their parents. Bruce and David and I had our family discussion beforehand. At the last minute, Peter said he wanted to go along. We could see nothing wrong with that, so he went. It was an ordinary night."

I could see that something horrible was coming.

"Well, Anne, on the way back, they had an off-the-road accident, up in the woods by the Flatirons. There were three boys. David had let the third boy drive the Jeep because he knew the lay of the dirt road they wanted to take out there. That boy was drunk and overturned the Jeep on some ice. Peter was killed."

Ruby took a deep breath. Her eyes didn't meet mine. "My husband accompanied Peter's body back to Germany. His parents said they forgave, and hoped that, if the boy who'd been driving had a drinking problem, he'd get help."

Ruby gave me a wan smile and then fastened her gaze on the door that Leah would soon be coming in through. "Of course, the guilt all of us felt was enormous. David took a leave-of-absence from school and stayed mostly in his room that winter. We had him see Dr. Warner. That's how Dick met us. And for a while, I saw a therapist Dick recommended for me.

"Why had my son let a drunk boy drive his Jeep? Of course, David was only sixteen, and his mental processes were not fully formed. And he was always trying to please his friends. After all, he was a teenager."

I thought back to Jane and Leah when they were teenagers, and remembered their impulsive, half-thought-out decisions.

"There was so much anguish. Our three boys walked around the house like they were hollow. But the other two never once, as far as I know, blamed David in word or gesture. That was very hard on our marriage. There was so much room for blame."

That, too, I knew something about.

"We all—the youngest and the oldest too—worried about David during those months. He let no one in. Then he let

Dick Warner in. Then he let his father in. Then one day in May he said he wanted to go to summer school and catch up.

"I don't know if David had been drinking that night. Perhaps his father knows. But David has never touched alcohol again. He graduated from high school, but he didn't go on to college like his brothers. He became a highly skilled automotive mechanic."

As Leah will become a travel agent.

"He has no bad habits, and leads a quiet life." Ruby sat quietly, and then said in conclusion, "As far as I can tell—and I honestly don't know how far I can tell—he's going to be all right. He'll be all right because he has accepted modifications to his life story. Ones imposed on him; ones he's chosen. And I don't blame myself anymore. That's only because it finally occurred to me one day that I didn't do anything to raise him to be in that Jeep accident." Her face became steady again. "I imagine you too have a lot you blame yourself for, Anne. You have an air of that about you. Guilt hurts just so, and it lasts for years. Especially when it's about our children. I just think lovely Leah ... well, you shouldn't blame yourself. You didn't raise your daughter to have schizophrenia."

"No. I did not raise Leah to have schizophrenia."

31

I told Len that he needed to give Evelyn a gift, since she'd worked long and hard for him as his secretary.
"Fine. Go get her something."
"I will not. You can get her something yourself."
"I don't know what that woman would want."
"Well, go to the bookstore in Cherry Creek, beside Hummel's, and get her a novel. Ask the woman who sells the books to choose something, and get her to gift wrap it."

He did just that, and brought himself home a book as well: *The Money Men*.

I looked at the cover, seeing apparently rich Wall Street types, looking full of energy and importance, very happy, very heroic. They were all Len's dreams come true.

He went through the book every free moment he had and then proceeded to explain money to me, while he drank his scotch in that chair of his. He explained a little more each evening. I suppose that was his way of sharing his dreams with me, not dreams as such, but facts he found fascinating, about banks, stocks (he intended to hire a broker next year), and so forth. I was so bored.

Len brought up Leah's five-thousand dollars at those lectures. I reminded him it was paying her little bit of rent until she started working at the travel agency. He said the point he was trying to make was that I'd given the money to Leah because I was impulsive and emotional.

Somehow that got connected in his mind to the idea that it was dangerous for me to own the ranch. And, if the truth be known, that I held the ranch over his and Jane's heads.

Each day when I was by myself, doing my little and often pointless chores, I thought about the ranch. I swept over the meadow in my mind's eye, and over all of it—lives grown, ripened, gone—I saw only dried hay stalks polished by the wind, sticking up here and there in the snow. In the winter, nothing was left of the Queen Anne's Lace. A summer not long ago, I'd come across a swath of broken-down grass by the plant, where some large animal had spent the night. But it too had moved on in the dawn. The fact of the matter was, the ranch no longer mattered to me as much as it did to Jane and Len. And it didn't seem, from what I could tell, that it mattered at all to Leah, beyond her memories of her horses and the telescope and collecting wild flowers. But Jane had a worshipful love of the ranch. It was the world's gift to her, and she was mindful of all that life there, requiring her proper care. Preserving the ranch was a life purpose. I didn't think she could have borne it if it had somehow, for some reason, passed on to someone else. I'd go so far as to say this: she loved the ranch as much as she loved her father.

MY MOTHER'S AUTOBIOGRAPHY

I didn't know where Alan fit into the picture. Maybe Jane was thinking they'd have children someday and her family could cherish the ranch after our family. But Alan at the ranch?

For Len, it seemed that the ranch was life-giving in a more complex way, going all the way back to his childhood of no money ever, a drunken father, a mother always sick, and now, his unclear future.

When I had discharged the gun into the trees that cold afternoon back in my woods, I had realized I would always survive. Because of his history and his character, I supposed, Len didn't have the option of that conclusion for himself. For that, I felt immensely sorry for him.

I felt so sorry for him that I decided to give him a gift for our thirtieth wedding anniversary, just around the corner. It would be the gift of security, as much as I was able to give that. I arranged for my lawyer—Len didn't know I had one—to draw up two documents.

On the morning of November 20th, I went to my hairdresser. In the afternoon, I shined up the gold on my engagement and wedding rings. At about five o'clock, I put the two Cornish hens in the oven and got into my good blue dress.

Just as the house was beginning to smell delicious from the hens, Len came home. Soon we were sitting in the living room, him with his pre-dinner scotch and I with an envelope. He didn't seem to notice that I was all dressed up, but he raised his eyebrows with some interest at the smile in my voice.

"Do you know how you keep saying that I can have anything I want?" I asked. "Well, here, you can too. Happy anniversary."

With a little surprised smile, Len cocked his head. He opened the envelope and studied the letter and then the document. Then he looked up at me. "This is a deed to fifty acres of the ranch, including the cabin and the other buildings."

"Yes. Jane gets the other half. The ranch will be all yours, yours and Jane's, free and clear of me."

He was solemn and still. We listened to nothing in particular; each waiting for what would come next.

Finally, he said, sincerely, "Thank you."

A week passed. Johnny Scannell gave Len two days off before his retirement date, so he could spend the Thanksgiving of '68 with his family. How unforeseeably kind.

At half past five, I stood in front of the darkening window in the dinette and thought, *What will I say to him, coming back from his office for the last time? What will he say, coming in the door?*

Then Len was pulling up and coming in with gifts. He had tears in his eyes.

"How did it go?" I asked, fumbling.

"Well, it's over now." A smile, brave and bitter. Not a big one.

"Let me take those so you can get your coat off. What are they?"

He blinked down his tears, and his smile relaxed. "The boys gave me a beautiful Pendleton plaid shirt to wear up at the ranch. Real wool. Look at that red. And leather gloves, look at them."

"Oh, they are beautiful. Evelyn must have gotten them. Did they have a cake?"

"Yes, one of those flat ones, big enough that everyone got a piece. Evelyn cut it. Then they all shook my hand, even Johnny Scannell. That goddamn fool made a little speech about how I'd be missed, what a good dispatcher I was. Can you imagine that? And he called me 'Lenny-O.' Only the boys ever called me 'Lenny-O.'"

"Well, it's over now."

Len's eyes filled again. "I think I'll go downstairs for a minute."

Soon I heard him down there, talking. I supposed he was calling Jane. Sitting at his desk, calling Jane.

He's moved from one desk to another, I thought. Always a man with a desk. Men and desks. I'd never had a desk. I'd had a kitchenette table on Bellaire Street, a big round oak table at the ranch, and a dinette table in Crestmoor Park. But never a desk.

Then silence downstairs. Twice I heard him blowing his nose loudly, so I knew he was crying.

To be of some comfort, I went to the top of the stairs and said, "Alice called me. She and Charles are coming over tonight, after dinner."

His eyelids were puffy when he came up, but he was all smiles. "Charles? Charles and Alice? I think I'll put on my new plaid shirt."

"We're having your mother's ground-beef goulash, your favorite."

Still smiling at the thought of their coming over, Len patted me on the top of my head. "You're a good cook, Anne."

I ducked under his hand and pulled away. "Don't do that," I grumbled.

Alice brought Len a lemon meringue pie, which she handed him as we all stood in the hall. His face turned bright, like a boy's at the sight of a birthday cake. "Oh my, it's still warm," he said in delight as he handed it to me. "Cut it up and let's serve it to these good people."

Charles produced from under his arm a bottle of champagne. Len clapped his hands at the complete surprise.

But how did you open a bottle of champagne? Neither Len nor I had ever done it. As though he could read that on our faces, Charles took it over to the kitchen. We heard a pop, and Charles said, "I need a glass."

I put one under the foaming champagne and then took charge. I told the three of them to go to the living room. I heard Len say, "Charles, come sit in my chair."

"Oh no, you're the guest of honor in your own home," Charles said. "This is your moment." He paused, adding, "So you've retired early, Len. Congratulations."

"Well, there's the good and the bad of it," Len said, almost under his breath.

"Well, there was the good and the bad of Indonesia."

"You don't say."

"That's one of the reasons we moved back stateside."

Len's eyebrows rose. *"Not just me?"* almost appeared on his lips.

"Honestly, Len, I envy you. Being your own man now, with your own appliance business. It'll be just like putting your feet in a good pair of shoes. You'll be running in no time. You're a lucky man."

Len had the expression of someone a priest had just laid hands on.

Then Charles brought out a long thin box. "We got this in Indonesia. It's for you, for this happy occasion." He got up and handed it to Len.

It was a letter opener—an ivory blade and a silver handle. It was possibly the most beautiful, sleek object I'd ever seen. The creamy ivory gleamed, and the simple, polished silver shown.

Len's hand shook as he held it up. He was clearly overwhelmed. "Charles, Alice, thank you," he said in a quivering voice.

Len was in awe, an almost holy look on his face. Well, maybe not *holy:* that sounded religious. He was just plain happy.

"Let's finish the champagne," Alice said, back in the moment. She walked from one to the other of us, pouring a bit in each glass. She added, "Now, we have great news of our own."

"What?" I asked, eager to hear her speak.

"Susan is going to study for six months in Florence, starting in January. Then she'll tour Europe for the rest of next summer."

Imagine, Susan in Europe! Not a sheltered child living with her parents in Indonesia, not a worried girl casting about in Colorado, but an independent young woman out seeing the world.

And Alice would be able to be my friend again.

We talked about how lovely it would be for Susan, what she would see, how accomplished she would become in art, in everything, really.

Jane was fine, I added quietly, and Leah was very fine.

As the Thatchers were leaving, Charles gave Len a hug. Was this the first bear hug Len had ever received? A bear hug from a robust man he admired in every way, not a routine handshake from a flabby manager who wished him ill. Len— the look on his face!—just then reminded me of a Saturn rocket rising mightily. So grand. Soon, they were saying in the news, a man would even land on the Moon.

Leah was at Ruby's home, to help with the big dinner. Len had told me Jane would be making her first Thanksgiving turkey. My husband was in his office in the basement.

I was at the counter in my kitchen, stuffing a chicken, about to stick it in the oven. This year, I was grateful for something more. I hadn't shot myself, but there was more. I was going to pull the trigger for my family, but I hadn't. Instead, I'd given myself mercy.

And I didn't need to have anybody even know it, or understand it, or approve of it. In a way, I shot the woods, and the woods hadn't noticed. They didn't notice me walking through them, ever. Just as they, and all that land, didn't notice Jane and Len. But I'm the only one who knew that. So in a way, I guessed, I was privileged.

Len came up, holding a greeting card he'd received Wednesday. On a garishly decorated plastic frame, which was supposed to look like real copper, were the words, "Dwell in Possibility." Written in small letters below was the saying's author: Emily Dickenson.

"What the hell does this mean?" he asked.

I took the card and turned it over. It was from Leah, who'd written, "Happy Retirement!!! I'm sorry for all the trouble I've caused you this year. It must have been very hard for you. I love you."

"That's quite nice," I said, touched. It was Leah caring about her father.

But the message of the card itself reflected Leah's typical obscurity.

"Call her up, why don't you?" I asked. "Ask her what it's supposed to mean."

Len paused, cocked his head, and then went over to the phone.

Ruby and Len said a few pleasantries about the holiday and the weather, and she passed the phone to his daughter, who was filling a pie crust with pumpkin.

"Leah, this is your father," Len began. "Your mother and I want to know what 'Dwell in Possibility' means."

He listened carefully.

"Oh. That's nice. Very nice. Well, thank you for the card. Have a good Thanksgiving, Leah. Goodbye."

Len turned to me. "Let me see if I can repeat this just right. She says it means, 'Live in the land where things might come true.'"

"That was nice of her."

"Yes, it was nice," Len said.

"How about this: 'Dwell in Possibility' can be the motto of the Mile-High Washing Machine Rental."

"Maybe I can get a sign made to put on the wall downstairs."

32

"Jane called this afternoon. You and I need to have a discussion," Len said.

I was putting my sack of groceries on the counter, and I had been about to say, *We're having T-bone steaks for dinner.* "What did she have to say?"

"She and Alan are getting married on December 26th."

"Oh. Well, I knew that was going to happen."

"She wants us to come. I told her we would."

"You told her without asking me first?"

"Don't you want to go to your daughter's wedding?"

"Now you're mixing everything up. You should have asked me first. You know you should have asked me first. And no, I am not going. You know I don't approve of Alan. You know that."

"Why?"

"Because I don't. And that's all I'm going to say. Period."

Len smacked his thigh with his open hand. "All right. Then we won't go. Period."

I put my head down and took a deep breath. Cornered into guilt. "You can always go without me, you know."

"I will not go without my wife."

Proud and resolute, because he was standing up against what he felt was wrong. Or he was afraid to go alone, surrounded by Alan's parents and—I supposed—lots of other people who looked different than he did, afraid to be asked by one guest and then another why his wife wasn't there (wasn't she feeling all right?), when they fully knew the answer. Len standing alone in a crowd, with nothing to do but smile some sort of smile.

"You know, you can be very selfish," he said, walking off.

For all of the next two days, Len and I didn't talk about Jane's wedding. But it wasn't as if we'd had a fight and were sulking. In fact, there hadn't even been a fight. We'd just hit a gray, concrete wall. That was exactly it.

Gray, concrete walls reminded me of apartment buildings' basement laundry rooms, which then led me to thinking of Len's new dedication to the Mile-High Washing Machine Rental. That first day working full time, he went downtown and came back with a fancy adding machine. The man at the office supply store had told him that, in the near future, there would be machines so small you could hold one in your hand while you did complicated calculations. You could even carry it around with you. Bored by that, I asked Len what was in the big box he'd just brought in with his dolly. He said that it was his very own mimeograph machine, because after all, he couldn't use the one in the dispatchers' office anymore.

When Len said "the dispatchers' office," he paused, looking at his hands. His voice broke once—just a tiny bit—when he said, "Well, I don't miss them anymore."

The second day, he went and bought a huge map of Denver, which he tacked to the wall opposite his desk in the basement. He would use variously colored pins to indicate apartment building locations, yellow meaning one thing, red another, green yet another.

"Now I'm going to sit down with the yellow pages and make a list of new buildings I can approach for business. Then, starting in January, I'm going to add nursing homes; imagine all the clothing they have to launder! 1969 is going to be a big year, and after that it's just going to get bigger and bigger." He thought, then added with bitterness, "I'll be worth ten times what Johnny Scannell can ever hope to make in a lifetime."

I felt sorry for him, missing United Airlines like that.

But my thoughts were really about Jane at that point. Surely, she didn't want *me* at her wedding. She had rejected me so long ago that I couldn't remember back that far.

Nonetheless, I couldn't put into words exactly why I would not go to my own daughter's wedding. Any other mother would have found the strength inside herself to be kind. I realized that fully. But my decision was a wrong I couldn't force myself to right. I shrank from Alan because he was not like us. And I felt that way because I was a flawed person; I was no Eleanor Roosevelt, preaching togetherness at the United Nations. Yes, "togetherness." Surely she didn't mean "unity." None of *her* offspring had married someone so different that it was the first thing you noticed.

I had not thought Jane would call me. But she did, in the middle of the third morning. Len wasn't in the house. I'd just finished washing the dishes from the evening before and from our breakfast. I hadn't yet had time to put my wedding rings back on, and I noticed how red and boney my naked hands were as I picked up the receiver.

"Good morning, this is Jane." Stilted and to the point.

"Good morning, Jane. How are you?"

"I understand you're not coming to my wedding. That's not at all surprising. But why are you keeping my father from coming?"

"Wait, I am not keeping your father from doing anything. He can go if he wants to. He's an adult."

"Yes, a lot of adults around there."

"Jane, please …"

Suddenly, in a turn unforeseen, she became tender. "You know, I've tried every way I can to get you to love me, for years now, and you won't."

"I didn't know you've been …" I looked at my ugly, unlovable hand holding up my connection to her. "I'm so sorry."

"How could you not know?" Jane's pleading voice was shrill.

I cast about in my mind for an answer. "You're a hard person to read, Jane."

"Well, you're a hard person to read too."

"What can we do?"

"You can come to my wedding."

"I can't come to your wedding."

"I'm closing the door, and I won't be opening it again." Now her voice was low, and a lifetime of resentment rolled through it. "Goodbye."

Jane said it politely, like folding up the blankets on her bed when she left home forever.

Hadn't I loved Jane? I moaned silently. *Hadn't I loved her?* That beaming baby, the most beautiful baby I'd ever seen. Then her running, squealing across the wet lawn, in her tiny red swimsuit, to grab her father around the legs. And her yellow cat, an ordinary yellow alley cat, so big she could barely lift him, her cat she fiercely called Dearest. Her rabbits—Jane was so tender to her tiny babies. Later, a fresh bouquet of wild flowers carefully chosen and arranged on the big ranch table each weekend. Jane walking, slowly and carefully through the meadow, face bent down, looking for Ute arrowheads, her collection of them—some shiny, black obsidian—kept in a tiny jewelry box. Jane hiking alone, finding old roads hewn by the settlers who had come after the Utes, rocky roads leading her far from home, down below the cliffs. Jane, twelve years old atop her chestnut mare, the bravest, proudest girl in the world. Jane and books, always books. Imagine—a fourteen-year-old girl reading the *Iliad* and *Poems from the Greek Anthology*. Then *Pride and Prejudice* and Anthony Trollope. Jane going around like a Victorian young lady saying, "It is my duty to be cheerful."

Was my love allowed no room for error?

I had loved my daughter, but I had not loved her the way she wanted to be loved. Or was it not the way she needed to be loved? No, I think I had in fact loved her the way she needed, because she turned out to be a young woman capable of her own kind of love, for a young man named Alan, whom I did not love, but whom she loved so much she wished to marry him. My daughter, who was shortly to be a bride. For whom that would be the happiest possible day of her life. That beautiful Jane, with her long dark-brown hair, her face beaming like when she was a baby, a bride holding a bouquet of fresh dewy roses, and the whole room smiling at her.

My daughter, whom I now would shower with gifts.

So, out of the bottom drawer of my jewelry box, I got out the gold locket my own mother had worn on her wedding day. I remembered their big, tinted wedding portrait, taken one day over fifty years ago, Mother wore the locket. Now its gold was pinkish. I opened the locket and saw tiny photographs of Pop and Mother. The locket had a long, heavy, gold-plated chain. I hadn't worn it the day I married, because Len and I had eloped, to save our parents money.

I wrapped the necklace in a handkerchief and put it on the side of my dresser. From my chest of drawers, I got out the document giving Jane the other half of the ranch, and I put it by the locket and chain.

The next thing I did was go shopping at the Denver Dry Goods Company, where I bought Jane a set of pink satin bedsheets and pillow cases, a cookbook by James Beard, and a small sewing kit. I got her a small white photo album for wedding pictures, and a table-sized silver-plated frame for their formal portrait. The woman at the frame counter boxed them all together and wrapped them in elegant sateen paper.

When I got back home, I went down to the basement to ask Len if he wanted to go with me to Bohm-Allen to select a strand of pearls for Jane.

"Yes," he said, "I'll go with you."

"When? You're so busy."

"Thursday."

MY MOTHER'S AUTOBIOGRAPHY

Thursday morning, Len and I got dressed up and went downtown. This was a different Len than the one who'd bought my engagement ring years before. This time, middle aged, he looked a bit wistful, and he had a genuinely generous smile. The salesman who greeted us was young and, it turned out, recently married himself. He seemed happy to help us.

Len picked out the strand. And the pearls he chose were stunning. They were not large and not small; they were an unusual middle size, one that would make a person look twice. The pearls' color was complex, white with hints of pink and possibly gold, and a deep sheen. The strand was quite long and had a gold clasp mounted with its own pearl. The salesman suggested earrings for it, and what I considered the most feminine pair also caught Len's eye.

Imagine, Len selecting jewelry for a young woman.

This was a substantial purchase, but this time Len didn't comment that it was an investment. He said, instead, that Jane could give them to *her* daughter someday.

So, Jane would have children. Of course she would. Children who would not look like her. But an unexpected sweetness, really a complete surprise, passed through me as I thought of Jane pregnant, then a mother. I, a grandmother. Len, a grandfather.

Then Jane invited Leah. Leah told me she was confused, cautious about it. I asked her if she'd talked to Dr. Warner about the trip. She said that he thought it was a good idea, a little vacation before she started work at the travel agency, and a chance to mend—or at least understand better—an important relationship. And anyway, she was well enough now.

Part of Leah was, of course, excited about a trip, an airplane trip, to a place she'd never been before. And she'd never been to a wedding. She decided to buy a record set of all of Beethoven's symphonies as her gift.

Len said that Leah was, at twenty two, still eligible for his retiree airline passes, but that it would be impossible to get a pass seat during Christmas travel, except of course on Christmas Day itself. That was fine with Leah. And it occurred to me that, if I drove up to Boulder to get her, then down and across Denver to the airport and finally back home, a lot of Christmas Day would be used up, and Len and I wouldn't have to spend so much holiday-nonsense time together.

But the main thing was that family would be present for Jane at her wedding. Things had sort of worked out for the best.

33

Colorado snows usually last a day and are followed by sun, stillness, brilliant white banks, and blue skies. It's warm enough that the mailman might be wearing shorts and a leather vest over his shirt.

December 25th was a day like that, a day to drive. I loved the way the highway came upon Boulder all of a sudden, showing the red sandstone and the barrel tiles of the campus buildings. In a way, the University of Colorado was more beautiful than Stanford, which was just yellow sandstone. The darker rocks of the buildings here had been hewn from the adjacent Rocky Mountains, so you felt uncannily at home.

Leah was waiting for me with her blue United Airlines overnight bag.

"Merry Christmas!" we both said, with broad smiles.

"You've packed enough medication in case you get laid over for three or four days, haven't you?" I asked.

"Mother ... come into the kitchen and get a cup of coffee. I've made enough for both of us. Anyway, relax. My plane doesn't leave Stapleton until one o'clock."

"Leah, you're so in charge."

"Of course I am." She handed me a CU Buffs mug.

"But you're not going to smoke marijuana or drink with those medications, are you?"

"Ha! I told Dr. Warner I wouldn't."

"Are you telling me too?"

"Yes, I'm telling you. I'm telling you a lot of things today."

"Like what?"

"Like, for starters, I love you, Mother."

My eyes open wide, an open-mouthed smile on my face—she'd actually said that.

"I love you too."

"I know you do. You always have. Dr. Pauley and Mrs. Hunter were full of shit."

"Leah, don't talk that way."

"Oh, come on, Mother. They were so ACCUSATORY. Okay, nobody's perfect, nobody in the Hope family is perfect, right? We all know that by now. But they taught those students they treated to blame their parents for everything. What an easy way out."

And that was all that needed to be said about those two, ever again.

How I loved my daughter for thinking for herself.

"Are you looking forward to staying at Jane's house?" I asked.

"Oh yes. I think so. It'll be intense. But she's my big sister. I've tried to make her my big sister, anyway. Getting married is going to make her happy. It's what she's always really wanted. I just hope Alan likes me. But I'll be nice. Whatever happens, I'll be the nicest person in the world."

"Leah, this will be between you and them. What I think of them or what they think of me has nothing to do with your sister and her husband and you. You're to make your own way."

"Oh, I know that," Leah said matter-of-factly, as though that was not a profound insight for a person her age.

"Well, I have a Christmas present for you guys," Leah continued. She handed me a boxed object, wrapped in red paper. "Open it now."

Inside was the circle drawing that I'd made when Ruby had shown me how to draw.

"Ruby gave the picture to me," Leah explained. "She said you'd left it behind. So I framed your drawing at the U-Frame-It. It's pretty cool, isn't it?"

"It's just beautiful …"

"Ruby said you should hang it over your sofa."

Something I made, framed by my daughter, in the place of honor.

"Mother, don't cry." Leah sounded like a little girl. "And here's a bag of catnip for Morgan."

Leah was indeed like a girl. And that would continue, I supposed. The thought kind of made me happy. It was her stake in magic.

I was driving happy on the Boulder turnpike, happy that Leah and I were getting along so wonderfully well. Leah was in turns relaxed and enthusiastic, hunched down in her seat or enjoying the views.

We had arrived at the edge of the Plains, which were, of course, covered with snow. I saw a pair of brown-and-white antelope. They jumped on spring legs, running in a line parallel to the highway. Then one of them veered off, back in the direction of Boulder. The other stood there and watched. We sped past them.

"Mother, why did you hit me so much when I was a kid? It wasn't like that time with Father, but you did hit me a lot."

Guilt like a monster for that period of my life.

Then I felt the oddest release, to have it finally spoken calmly. In sanity. A chain popped. My daughter was freeing me from what I could never say myself.

"I am grateful to you, Leah."

"Why? You're not making any sense, Mother."

"You wouldn't understand. You've never been in charge of another person's life."

"Mother, why did you do it? Was I that awful?"

"You didn't deserve it in any way. Do you remember when you were at the hospital, and you kept saying, 'I don't know, I don't know'?"

"Yes …"

"Do you remember how you felt then?"

"Like I was in a cage, which was getting smaller."

"Leah, I had been in one too. For years. I had no one to tell it to, so I took it out on you. All I can say is that I'm so very, very sorry."

"You're not in there anymore, are you?"

"No. You tipped the cage over. Thank you, Leah."

"You're welcome."

"After your trip, I want you to head off in your own direction. Make your life in Boulder, or wherever you want."

I waited for her to say something, but she was quiet. "What else were you going to tell me today? You were going to tell me several things."

"Yeah, two things. First, that I love you, which I already said. And I do love you. But I also wanted to tell you—and it's about Jane and Alan—that you should 'Break on Through to the Other Side.' That's a rock song by the Doors."

"What does that mean?"

"You need to do some heavy thinking, Mother."

At Airport Departures, Leah leaned over, kissed me on the forehead, and said, grinning, "Think of me as your psychiatrist."

It was noon, and I drove homeward. I was in fact thinking hard, and wanted to be by myself. But of course, on Christmas Day everything in my neighborhood was closed, even Hummel's, even the library. There was no opportunity for public solitude.

So I headed to the house. I yelled "I'm back" down to Len in the basement, and got a cup of tea and a couple of cookies. Then I went, not really knowing why, to Jane's room. I closed the door behind me.

It was still her world, that room. White and girlish. I'd gone ahead and added the white afghan her Kaiser grandmother] had crocheted for her. I made a mental note that Jane's yellow gingham curtains had become a little droopy, in need of laundering. Her bookshelf was pretty empty, but the Iliad was still there. Maybe she'd really wanted it, but hadn't had room in either of her two suitcases. *I should send it to her*, I thought.

I sat in her white wicker chair. But even with the hot tea, I suddenly felt cool. So I took my mother's afghan off Jane's bed and covered my lap and legs with it.

The three of us there. Elizabeth Jenovai Kaiser, illiterate. Anne Kaiser Hope, who read ladylike books like *The Prophet*. And now Jane Hope Wong, librarian.

Elizabeth Jenovai Kaiser's long trip across the Atlantic, her trip through Germantown, her husband in the factory, her daughter Anne in the factory, slowly climbing up and up, to Crestmoor Park and Stanford. A young man who had, as a tiny child, made the long trip across the Pacific Ocean, to San Francisco, to UCLA. There was no room for shame at any of this. Shame was unworthy. Shame was twisted.

That I should have the strength to cross an ocean.

But there was another journey anyone could make. It was the journey inward. A long time ago I had seriously wondered if I existed. Across the years I'd moved further and further inward as I had swept the crumbs from a kitchenette table, then later from a dinette table. As I'd cared for an old, dying cat. As I'd picked pieces of a broken light bulb off the beige carpet in an El Camino Real motel. I had pointed a gun to my head and afterward thought the matter over slowly, sitting at my big oak table, me alone, surrounded by woods.

The gun. Aiming it at nothing, then putting it aside. The end, in a way, of my lifetime of fighting. The beginning of the end, at least. I was not fighting Leah now, and she was returning to me. I was not fighting Len, and I was receiving from him what appeared to be simple gratitude.

I had a thought like a crystal: *Why should I fight Jane?*

Couldn't I choose instead to respect her? Respect her for making up her own mind about life, rightly proud of her judgment and values? That would mean respecting her choices. Her one choice. Yes, *that*. And I could. I was doing it at this very moment, sitting in her room. Mingling my thoughts with the ghost of my mother, Elizabeth. I did not know if Jane would ever return to me, but I could stop fighting her, couldn't I?

That evening, I said to Len, "You know, I've decided to respect Jane. I owe her that."

Len said, "That's right."

December 26th, 1968 was a Thursday. Jane and Alan would have a long weekend for a sort of stay-at-home honeymoon. Classes at the University of Minnesota wouldn't start for another two weeks after that. If it snowed Minnesota-hard, they could stay at home the whole time, cozy.

They'd be married at City Hall in the late morning and then go to a Chinese restaurant with Alan's parents, grandparents, brothers, and Leah for a wedding feast, Chinese style. Then they'd all return to the apartment, where Alan and Jane Wong would open their various gifts. Eventually they'd be alone, except for Leah. They had a cot for her in their study. Leah had told me all these details before she left.

Len and I didn't know anything more. Our day was long. All we did was imagine. I imagined noisy, happy guests, perhaps even talking Chinese.

I wondered if Jane had worn the locket. If she'd worn the pearls. If she liked the pearls. If the deed to the ranch had made her like me for a moment.

Seven o'clock in the evening, we were sitting in the dinette, Len and I. The phone rang. We'd agreed Len would answer. It was Jane. Her father talked to her, told her how proud he was of her. He congratulated Alan.

Then Jane asked to talk to me. Yes, Jane asked for me. She had both tears and coolness in her voice. I spoke, and had tears in mine. I asked her what her dress looked like. It was red velveteen with white lace. Then, clearly awed, she told me about the jewelry her in-laws had given her: a jade-and-gold bracelet, earrings, a ring, and a magnificent jade pendant with a thick, bright gold chain. She didn't mention our jewelry.

"I hope you'll be happy, Jane, for the rest of your life, with your husband. I'm proud of you for choosing Alan." I caught my breath, heard only silence. "I'm proud of you for your studies, for being in graduate school. I know you'll be happy, both of you. And I hope both of you want to come to our home, to be part of our family."

I didn't know, but hoped, that someday she'd accept that I was, just now, being sincere.

The sigh Jane let go of was short, bitter. I imagined her eyes were closed.

She quickly asked me if I wanted to speak to Alan.

"Yes, I'd really like to speak with Alan, thank you," I said.

Suddenly, I felt like it was all the moments of my life squeezed together.

"I bet Jane is beautiful," I said to Alan. "They say a woman is most beautiful on her wedding day."

"Oh, I remember when Jane's been even more beautiful," he said.

"Well, I know you'll take good care of her." I spoke from the bottom of my heart.

"I will," he said. "And she'll take good care of me."

I hadn't thought of that at all, had I?

I couldn't think of what to say next.

"Well ..." Alan said. Just like he was smirking. I could almost see it.

I still told him that I hoped they would have a long, happy marriage, that they'd be part of our lives, we part of theirs.

I hoped that someday, he, too, would accept I was being sincere.

We said goodbye. Nobody said, "I love you."

Then Len and I sat back in our places in the living room.

"Did she wear the pearls?" Len asked.

"Oh, yes," I lied. "And she liked them because they were your idea."

He got a big smile on his face.

Author's Note

Starting in the late 1940s, the concept of the schizophrenogenic mother was popular in psychiatric literature and practice. In the early 1970s, Seymour Kety published an influential adoption study suggesting the concept was invalid, but the model of the destructive mother that molded schizophrenia in her offspring continued to be popular even in the early 1980s.

The National Alliance for the Mentally Ill (NAMI) traces its origins to Harriet Shetler and Beverly Young, who lived in Madison, Wisconsin. Both had sons diagnosed with schizophrenia, and the two women were sick and tired of taking the blame for their sons' illnesses. The first meeting of NAMI was held in 1979.

Anne Hope attended meetings of NAMI in Denver in the 1980s, and Leah Hope spoke at many meetings, about her life and that of her mother's.

Acknowledgments

Above all, I thank my Argentinian stepsister, Amalia Marcet. I simply could not have written *My Mother's Autobiography* without her kind and encouraging help. Her knowledge of human nature has both explored and affirmed characters and events throughout the novel.

I owe deep thanks to Robert Freedman, MD, Editor-in-Chief Emeritus of *The American Journal of Psychiatry*, who has gone over this book twice. Across the years, he has taught me lucidity, both in writing and in living.

Thanks to Andre Dubus III, who read early sections of this novel in 2017. His great enthusiasm for them was pivotal in finding my courage to continue writing.

Matthew Limpede gave the manuscript two wonderful developmental critiques.

David Dobbs, Robert Phillips, and Elizabeth Holtze have been diligent, insightful readers.

I thank Steven Dworetsky, MD, for quietly encouraging patience in my long journey to publish.

My long-standing writing group—called both humorously and affectionately—The She-Thugs, has always put things, both written and worldly, in focus for me. The Thugs gave my book, in its various parts, first-rate critiques; I thank Windy Lynn Harris, Paulette Fire, Andrea Bobotis, Natalee Tucker, Julie Comins Pickrell, Ainsley McWha, and Twila Newey.

The Lighthouse Writers Workshop of Denver has, for years now, given me instruction, inspiration, and sheer respect for my efforts. Thank you.

My book has found a good home at Jaded Ibis Press. I thank in particular Elizabeth Earley, its publisher; my editor, Seth Fischer; and the skilled and hardworking production staff led by Carmen Peters.

And finally, I thank Cindy Rasmussen and all my other friends, for their often-daily support as I wrote this, my debut novel, which I am publishing at the age of seventy-nine.